The Alchemy of Words

Beginner's Guide to Colorful Writing

Madison Pike

Foreword

Welcome to the exhilarating journey of creative writing! Within the pages of this book, you will embark on a thrilling exploration of the art and craft of writing, unlocking the secrets to crafting compelling stories that captivate readers and leave a lasting impact.

Each chapter is a gateway to a new realm of knowledge, offering a treasure trove of techniques, insights, and inspiration. From the very beginning, we delve into the fundamental aspects of creative writing, understanding the intricacies of different genres and the importance of cultivating a writing routine that sparks your imagination and fuels your passion.

As we progress, we dive into the depths of finding inspiration, discovering how personal experiences and the power of observation can breathe life into your stories. We unleash the potential of prompts and exercises, igniting your creativity and infusing it with boundless energy.

But what are stories without memorable characters? Fear not, for we delve into the art of character creation, crafting multidimensional individuals who will step off the page and into the hearts of your readers. We explore the nuances of dialogue, mastering the art of capturing natural speech patterns and using words to convey subtext and emotion. And we unravel the secrets of character arcs and motivations, ensuring that your characters grow, evolve, and leave a lasting impression.

No story is complete without a compelling plot, and we unravel the threads of storytelling, constructing narratives that keep readers on the edge of their seats. We understand the importance of story structure, the infusion of conflict and tension, and the strategic use of plot devices and twists that leave readers gasping for more.

In the realm of descriptive prowess, we venture into the craft of crafting vivid settings, where sensory details transport readers to enchanting worlds. We learn to create environments that feel authentic and evocative, using settings as a powerful tool to convey mood and atmosphere.

As we navigate the realm of storytelling, we master the art of point of view, understanding its impact on characterization and reader immersion. We explore different narrative perspectives, choosing the right point of view to bring our stories to life, and harnessing this perspective to create a deeply engaging reading experience.

Language becomes our ally as we uncover the power of words. We develop a distinctive writing style, a voice that echoes with your unique creative essence. We embrace the beauty of figurative language and literary devices, infusing our prose with vivid imagery and emotional resonance. And we polish our writing through the fine art of editing and revision, refining our work to shine brilliantly.

Engaging dialogue becomes our forte as we capture the essence of natural speech patterns, infusing our conversations with authenticity and vitality. We delve into the depths of subtext and emotion, utilizing dialogue as a powerful vehicle for character development and storytelling. And we strike a delicate balance between dialogue and narrative description, creating a harmonious symphony of words that guides readers through our narrative.

In the realm of pacing and time management, we learn to control the narrative tempo, balancing action and reflection to create a dynamic reading experience. We explore the power of flashbacks and foreshadowing, wielding them as tools to heighten suspense and deepen the narrative layers.

Research becomes our ally as we enhance our writing with authenticity and real-world elements. We discover effective research techniques, incorporating factual knowledge seamlessly into our fictional worlds. And we navigate the common pitfalls and errors, ensuring that our writing remains polished, accurate, and immersive.

But our journey doesn't end there. We delve into the importance of self-editing, equipping ourselves with the techniques to strengthen our plots, characters, and language. And we embrace the transformative power of seeking feedback and working with editors, opening ourselves to collaboration and the opportunity for growth.

Summary

Chapter 1: Introduction to Creative Writing

The Art and Craft of Creative Writing

Creative writing can be a fascinating journey for both writers and readers. It takes them into the world of storytelling and imagination. The writer's pen is an expression tool that weaves a tapestry of thoughts and emotions.

Creative writing, at its heart, is an art that promotes communication and self-expression. The medium allows writers to delve deep into their souls and extract fragments from their experiences, their dreams and their observations. Writers use their own personal inspiration, like a painter using a palette, to develop characters, settings and narratives which resonate with readers.

Creative writing is more than just a form of art. It is a skill that requires dedication, discipline and the development of new skills. This requires an in-depth understanding of grammar and language. The writers embark on an endless journey to learn, exploring plot structure, dialogue, character development and other aspects of writing.

As writers balance imagination with technique, the art and craft of writing creatively intertwine. By using carefully chosen words and images, authors create vivid pictures, which allow readers to feel as if they are in the characters' shoes, experience the magic of the worlds described, or even breathe it.

Writers revise and edit their works, polishing them until they shine with clarity and resonance. The writers know the importance of revising and re-reading their work, as the initial draft is only a rough sketch. They also understand that it's important to add layers, refine details, and transform flaws into beautiful strokes.

The art of writing creatively involves the construction of intricate plots that are built on conflict, tension and suspense. The vast array of genres has its own conventions and expectations. They explore the mysteries of life, travel to fantastical worlds or discover the truths about human nature.

This journey is for aspiring writers who embrace the craft and art of writing creatively with an open heart and a curious mind. The writers immerse their minds in literary masterpieces and study the methods used. They are inspired by the brilliant work of the past. The writers create sacred places and dedicate routines to weave writing into their daily lives.

Creative writing is an art that invites you to explore a universe of endless possibilities. Words become paintbrushes, and tales are weaved with imagination. This is a call that demands courage, vulnerability and an unwavering pursuit of beauty and truth. As writers begin this exciting journey, they find that their voices have the ability to ignite the minds of others, touch the hearts of readers, and make a lasting impression on human narrative.

It is as if the art of writing creatively flows like a stream of water through a rich tapestry. The writer's creativity and technical skill are combined in a harmonious way to produce a beautiful symphony.

Writers embark on an adventure of exploration in this world of fluid creativity. They explore the unknown territories of their hearts and minds. The writers dive into their own experiences and draw on the vivid emotions, memories, vibrant sensations, etc. that are there. They dip their pen into the river that is themselves, and allow its currents carry them to new levels of self-expression.

The words cascade down like a torrent, splashing around and bringing life to the page. Each sentence carries the writer's unique voice, which whispers secrets or evokes laughter. The narrative is like a river that flows through different landscapes. It carries readers with it, allowing them to be immersed in the world created by the author's visions and dreams.

Creative writing requires a delicate dance of inspiration and technique. The writers refine their craft, expanding their toolkit and refining the literary palette. The writers weave plots together with precision and finesse, integrating characters, conflict, and resolutions seamlessly. Like a ripple on the surface of the water, each paragraph propels the plot forward and engages the reader.

Writers paint vivid landscapes with the help of their language. They create a panorama in front of the reader. They describe with vivid strokes the smell of flowers in bloom, the warmth from a summer wind, or even the melancholy of rainy days. They create a sensory tapestry that invites readers to immerse themselves in the world of a story.

The dialogue moves across the page like a stream, giving the interactions of the characters more depth. Readers can hear subtle emotion and nuances in the voices of the characters through their dialogue. The ebbs and flows of the human conversation are orchestrated in this symphony, giving life to the characters, and injecting authenticity into the story.

Creative writing allows time to be fluid and bend or twist according to the narrative. As if a cascading waterfall plunges readers back into history, foreshadowing gently suggests what is to come, much like the ripples of water on the surface. This writer creates a rhythm to keep readers turning pages and captivated by the story's flow.

The art and craft behind creative writing are a journey both the writer and reader take together. The magic of story-telling and the fluidity in words combine to form an unforgettable bond. The writer dances his pen across the page and the reader follows along with their feelings as they rise and fall.

The writer's voice is a constant in this landscape, which leads readers to a journey of discovery, illumination, and enjoyment. In this world, imagination is free to run, boundaries are blurred, and the power of the written word transcends space and time. Immerse yourself in the creative process, let your imagination run wild, and allow the flow of words to take you on a journey of storytelling and self-expression.

Creative writing can be compared to a river that flows constantly, with ideas and thoughts colliding and forming currents. This creates a flow of imagination and exploration for both the writer and the reader. The landscape is fluid, with words intertwining and meandering. It creates a smooth flow which captivates all the senses.

The writer is a navigator in this world of fluidity, charting its course with an even hand. The writer, like a river, shapes a story by shaping characters, plotlines and giving every sentence meaning and purpose. The narrative cascades through the paragraphs or chapters with each keystroke of the keyboard.

It is a natural process that ebbs, flows and reflects the rhythm of our lives. The art of creative writing is like a tide, as it moves between discipline and inspiration. Writers surrender to the flow of the tide, and allow their ideas to run free, without being restricted by logic or convention. In this space, innovation flourishes. Unconventional ideas are born and the imagination blooms.

As a river gains momentum as it flows downstream, so too does the art of creative writing. It is built on a solid foundation of skill and knowledge. The study of structure, language and technique is a must for writers who want to improve their skills. The art of pace is taught, and they learn when to move quickly or linger to allow emotions to settle.

The language becomes an emotional current, carrying the author's intention and that of the reader. Words create an enchanting symphony within the soul of the reader, like the soft babble of the brook and the rush of the waterfall. The sentences flow smoothly, taking the reader on a journey of sensory experiences, including sights, sounds and smells. The narrative is laced with metaphors and similes that evoke vivid images and enhance the emotional attachment.

The dialogue emerges as tributaries that branch off the main stream of the story. The dialogue is lively, like a dance on the surface. It reveals the complexity of the human relationship and character. Characters' words have their own fluidity, reflecting personalities, motives and dynamic relationships. The reader is immersed into the conversation through dialogue. They can hear the subtext and cadence.

Time becomes fluid as the narrative moves, bending to the requirements of the plot. Flashbacks ripple in the flow, immersing the reader into the past while foreshadowing gives hints of the future. This writer creates a rhythmic flow that allows readers to easily navigate through the story, with a sense of surprise and suspense.

This continuous fluidity of creative writing allows it to transcend its borders, transporting the reader into new worlds and perspectives. It also transports them to new emotions. This is an invitation for readers to surrender themselves to the flow of imagination and let go of their constraints. The writer and the reader are both part of this powerful current as they embark together on a fluid journey.

Let your writing flow as a river will carry stories, emotions, and ideas downstream. Allow the flow of creativity to lead you and allow your imagination to ripple across the page, making an impression on your reader's hearts.

Understanding Different Writing Genres

It is like navigating an ever-changing and vast river. Each current has its own unique qualities and allure. Genres are like tributaries that merge into the main stream. They offer diverse paths to both readers and writers, creating an endless landscape of literary possibilities.

Imagine yourself standing on the edge of a river, with the different genres of literature flowing past you. You step into the water and are immediately embraced by a first current, which is the world of fiction. The vastness of this river stretches from historical fiction with its tapestry rich in the past to speculative fantasy, which is where the imagination has no limits. You will be carried along by the current through stories of romance, mysteries, fantasy and science fiction. Each story has its own currents, which will entice you to explore their worlds.

You will come across another branch as you travel through the river of words: non-fiction. The river of words here flows in a new rhythm that guides you to the worlds of memoir, biography and informational works. The current offers a window into real life, offering knowledge and insights that will leave a lasting impression on the reader. This river carries you through historical accounts, discoveries of science, and untold tales of extraordinary individuals. It is a treasure trove of knowledge and inspiration.

The river continues to flow downstream and reveals another current, poetry. The river flows elegantly and deeply, bringing the elegance of language with it. This lyrical world is a place where words flow like a waterfall, evoking emotions and vivid images. Through the flow of the verse, poetry explores human experiences and connects hearts and minds. The poetry embraces metaphor, symbolism and rhythm. This allows writers to express profound ideas and emotions.

You will encounter drama and playwriting as you move along the continuous current. This is an energetic current that's bursting with performance power and energy. The words dance on the page, bringing life to characters, dialogue and stage directions. The current encourages writers to examine the human condition by using dialogue, conflict and tension. This is an area where the flow of words can become a drama, with the audience or reader becoming a part of the action.

Each genre has its own flow, which merges and diverges, creating a constantly changing landscape of literary expression. The tapestry is made up of the stories, the emotions and the insatiable thirst for storytelling. Both writers and readers have the chance to immerse themselves in the emotions and currents which resonate with them.

Genres evolve over time, just as a river changes its shape to fit the terrain. As new currents form, they combine elements from different genres to create hybrids which challenge conventional storytelling and push the boundaries. It is a river that flows and changes with the literary landscape.

Accept the fluidity and flow of different genres. Allow the currents to guide you and invite you into the depths that are fiction, nonfiction, poetry and drama. Let the unique characteristics of each genre carry you along on a voyage of exploration, illumination, and creativity.

It's like learning to navigate a river of writing styles that flows through an array of different literary forms. The ever-changing, fluid river of writing genres offers endless possibilities to both writers and readers. Let the river of genres guide us as we begin this journey.

Imagine yourself on the bank of a river, the calm water beckoning you to move forward. You step into the water and the world of fiction is embraced. This current carries you to a variety of worlds. It takes you into the fantasy realms, intricate webs and romance. It is a current that carries you through a story, with vivid characters and captivating plots. The imaginative settings and places transport you into familiar and fantasy worlds.

The river splits as you continue to navigate, and you will find yourself in the non-fiction current. The tributary is a river of knowledge, truth and real life stories. This tributary takes you to the heart of history and science and offers insights that are resonant with human nature. Non-fiction is a current that illuminates our world, bringing facts, stories, and pursuit of knowledge to the surface.

Continue along this path and you will encounter the poetry current, where words cascade like waterfalls with images, rhythms, and emotions. The current of poetry flows through the river, revealing metaphors' power, verse cadences, and human expression. The lyrical, the abstract and the fluidity of the language are all embraced in this work.

The river becomes wider as it flows downstream. Drama and playwriting are revealed. The current is a whirlwind of energy, magic, and human interaction. This current takes you on a journey through conflict dynamics, stage directions and storytelling. This current, like a compelling production, invites both readers and actors to interact with the words, embody characters, and bring their stories alive.

We see how, as we travel along the river, each genre merges and intertwines, resulting in new subgenres and forms of story telling. It adapts to reflect the changing nature of literature, and readers' diverse tastes. The river invites us embrace genres as they ebb, flow, and change. It also allows us to explore currents which resonate with our interests and passions.

Let us then surrender to these currents and let the fluidity in understanding the different genres of writing carry us. Explore the unique currents in fiction, poetry, drama and non-fiction. Discover their beauty and power. We will let the river lead us as we explore the fluidity of the genres and go on an inspirational literary journey.

It's like immersing yourself in a river of creative expression where currents converge and intertwine in an ever-changing, flowing dance. Imagine yourself standing on the edge of a river, watching the genres flow through an array of landscapes, inviting you into its depths.

The current of imagination will carry you along as you enter the river. Fiction encompasses many genres with their own unique flavor, like a river current. You are swept along as you explore the world of fantasy where mythical beings and magical realms come to life. You are guided through currents of mysteries, where puzzles and enigmas are revealed. You are carried along romantic streams, where hearts and love intertwine. Fiction is an ever-changing realm of imagination that transports both the writer and reader into unexplored territories.

You will notice another current as you move further down the river. This is non-fiction. The non-fiction current runs in parallel with its fiction counterpart and offers a grounded look at reality. It offers an array of genres with a constant and informative flow.

These include biography, history and science. The current of non-fiction is an excellent source of information and illumination, taking you on a journey through real life narratives, historic events, scientific discoveries and personal development. Non-fiction is a current that imparts knowledge and wisdom, flowing in harmony with the genres. It enriches our understanding of life.

While you are navigating the meandering water, a new current appears--the poetry current. This is a lyrical stream, where the words flow and ripple, carrying images and emotions. Poetry is like a gentle and melodic flow that invites us to appreciate the beauty of language, metaphor, and rhythm. You are encouraged to dive deep into human experience by surrendering to the cadence and gentle rhythm of the verses. It is a current that cascades raw emotions, sensory landscapes and vivid words to create an immersive experience.

You will encounter drama and playwriting further downstream. The current is full of theatricality and energy, mirroring a fast-moving river. This current carries a sense of dialogue and performance, with stories meant to be performed on a stage. This current combines the theatrical conventions, characterization and conflict to create a unique way of telling stories. Drama invites both readers and actors to experience the dynamic of human relationships and the tension created by dialogue. It also allows them to learn about the nuances of stage direction and plot.

You can see the interplay of these genres as you follow their flowing, continuous currents. As the landscape and tastes of readers change, the river of genres changes and adapts. This is a vibrant ecosystem, where hybrids and new storytelling techniques are created by combining elements from different genres.

Let's immerse ourself in the fluidity and flow of different genres. We will explore fiction, nonfiction, drama, poetry and more by letting the currents lead us. Let the currents carry you, opening your mind to new possibilities and inviting you to embrace the constantly changing landscape of literary expression. We hope to find inspiration, enlightenment and joy as we explore the ever-changing landscape of literary expression.

The Importance of Developing a Writing Routine

Writing routines are important because they allow you to tap into a continuous flow of creative inspiration, where structure and discipline blend seamlessly with fluidity. In establishing a writing routine, writers can achieve a balance that allows their words and ideas to flow freely, as if a river was weaving across the landscape of imagination.

Imagine you are at the edge of the river, watching the constant flow of water. A writing routine is like a river that follows its course with unwavering resolve. It provides a constant outlet for creativity. You can create a writing routine by immersing yourself into its rhythm and knowing you will progress each day.

A writing routine is like the river currents that form the landscape. It shapes you as a writer. The routine creates a space and time that is dedicated to writing, allowing the writer's mind to be primed for creative thinking. The flow is constant, providing a feeling of familiarity and stability in an often unpredictably unpredictable world. It becomes a constant, encouraging writers, to be present regularly and honor their dedication to the craft.

You will find, as the river guides you, that showing up is effortless. It becomes a part of daily living, woven into your fabric. You can tap into your creative side consistently and nurture the seed of an idea.

Inspiration finds its voice in the writing routine. A routine is like a river that brings with it a wealth of life. It's fertile soil for new ideas. The muse can be summoned by the regular practice of writing, almost as though the river were whispering secrets in the writer's ears. It is the routine that allows the writer to translate those moments of inspiration into words.

You will begin to see its transformational power as you move through your routine. The routine will make you a better writer, just as the river shapes the landscape over time. The routine allows you to improve your writing skills with every passing day. It instills perseverance and reminds you to be consistent in your efforts.

You find empowerment and comfort in this rhythmic, continuous writing. This sacred place becomes your sanctuary where you surrender to your creative flow. It gives you a sense purpose and direction even if inspiration is ebbing and flowing.

By embracing the value of a regular writing schedule, you will understand that creativity does not come and go but is a constant. The writing routine is like a river, which flows continuously, reminding you that the words that you write have the ability to change the world, touch the hearts of others, and spark change. In your commitment to a writing routine, you can unlock your full creative potential.

A writing routine can be compared to a constant, fluid stream of creative inspiration, in which structure and discipline blend seamlessly with spontaneity. A writing routine is like a constant current of water that never stops flowing. It guides writers' thoughts and words in a smooth, unbroken flow.

Imagine yourself standing on the edge of a river, watching the water slither through the land. You step into the water and become immersed, feeling its currents embrace you. This invites you to surrender your writing to rhythm.

A writing routine is like the flow of a river. It provides writers with a solid foundation. The routine creates a feeling of purpose and stability, and a time and place for writers to write. The routine, which is a set of rules for committing to the art, becomes an important guide that encourages writers to show up regularly and be engaged in their creative process.

The writing becomes an extension of you as the river moves along. This is an ongoing, fluid practice that will become a part of your everyday life. This creates a flow, similar to the sound of the water lapping against the bank of a river, which allows you immerse in writing. It becomes a part of who you are as a writer, and allows you to tap effortlessly into the creative flow.

Inspiration finds its voice in the fluidity and flexibility of your writing routine. The routine is like a river that has many tributaries. It channels all the different sources of inspiration to influence your writing. The routine becomes an inspiration vessel, almost as though the river whispered stories, characters and brilliant moments directly to your mind. It becomes a channel, an instrument that channels the creative currents onto paper.

You will be amazed at the power of transformation that occurs when you allow your routine to flow. The routine will shape you over time as a writer, just like the river shapes the landscape. The routine cultivates your discipline by honing and developing your writing skills. It encourages growth and reminds you to be persistent in your efforts.

You can find refuge in the flowing, continuous rhythm of your writing. It is a place that provides solace, empowerment, and focus. This routine becomes your sanctuary, where you surrender to your emotions and thoughts. This routine teaches you the importance of being consistent and how to enjoy exploration. This routine gives you a purpose and a direction even when inspiration seems to be calm.

By embracing the value of writing a routine, you are embracing the constant flow of creative energy. The rhythm of your writing routine is the key to harnessing and nurturing inspiration. This continuous commitment will unlock your full creative potential, and allow it to merge with your unique perspectives.

It is important to develop a routine for writing. This can be compared with immersing yourself in a river flowing, where the creativity flows continuously and fluidly, guiding writers towards their goals. A writing routine, like the currents of a river, creates an uninterrupted flow that combines structure with inspiration, propelling writers on their creative journey.

Imagine yourself standing by the edge of the river, the gentle undulating flow of the current beckoning you. The current will embrace you as you enter the river. It will guide your movement and merge with your rhythmic creative process. The fluidity of the river represents a daily writing practice that is a part of you.

A writing routine is like the currents of a river. It offers consistency and stability. This dependable flow will carry you through all the highs and lows in your creative journey. A writing routine creates dedicated space and time for writing. This ensures that creativity remains the priority. It is the constant current of your life that keeps you moving forward even when distractions and doubts are present.

Inspiration flourishes in the continuous flow of writing. Daily engagement in the craft is like tributaries that feed the river. It allows ideas to grow and develop. It becomes a channel, guiding the inspiration to the written word. The routine encourages an intuitive and disciplined dance as your ideas flow effortlessly onto the page.

You will be amazed at the power of transformation that occurs when you allow your routine to flow. The routine is like the current of a river that shapes the landscape it passes through. The routine instills a sense of discipline and refines your writing skills by requiring you to practice consistently. The routine fosters resilience by nurturing your ability to overcome obstacles and navigate through challenges. It is the routine that will keep you grounded, support your growth and help you achieve your writing goals.

You find refuge in the flowing, continuous rhythm of your daily writing. This is a place where self-expression and creativity flourish. The writing routine provides solace in the midst of chaos, just as the current of a river brings peace. The writing routine becomes sacred, an oasis where you can be immersed in your emotions and thoughts without distractions. This routine allows you to embrace your creativity and tap into your wellspring.

It is important to recognize that a regular writing schedule helps you cultivate and nurture your creativity. To recognize the writer's journey as a fluid, ever-evolving process and to understand that constant engagement with your craft will unlock your creative potential is to acknowledge the importance of having a writing routine. The fluidity in your writing allows you to merge with currents of creativity, and transform your ideas into tangible, expressive expressions.

Step into your routine and immerse yourself. Take in the rhythmic flow that drives your creativity. Surrender to the flow and allow your imagination to run wild. Allow the writing ritual to be your guiding current, propelling you towards creative goals. You will embark on an exciting journey of artistic expression and self-discovery.

Chapter 2: Finding Inspiration

Exploring Personal Experiences as Writing Material

Writing about personal experiences is like dipping your pen in a stream of emotions and memories that flow continuously. This allows them to influence and enrich your writing with depth and authenticity. Personal experiences are like the currents of a river, flowing effortlessly and providing rich material from which to draw inspiration. This gives writers' work an intimacy and resonance.

Imagine yourself standing at the edge of the river, watching the reflections in the water. You can immerse in the currents and dive deep into your past experiences as you swim through the river. The continuous flow of the river is a wellspring that writers can use to transform personal stories into compelling narratives.

Personal experiences are like the currents of a river that meander across diverse terrains. They offer a vast canvas for story-telling. Personal experiences become fertile soil from which to cultivate narratives. They infuse them with raw emotions, vivid detail, and nuanced perspective that can only be provided by personal encounters. Memories, challenges, successes, and relationships are all woven into your writing by the current of personal experience.

In the fluidity and authenticity of their personal stories, writers can find inspiration. Personal stories are like tributaries that merge into the main stream to form a singular voice. The writers use their personal experiences to create a unique voice and perspective. Readers connect to the authenticity of the writer's writing, because they can relate to the real emotions and situations that are portrayed.

You will be amazed at the power of transformation that comes from surrendering to your own current. This flow can be a reflection tool, allowing writers to understand and explore their journey. This exploration allows writers to uncover universal truths and illuminate the common aspects of human nature. As readers connect with the author's honesty and vulnerability, they find inspiration and comfort.

As the river shapes and molds the landscape it passes through, so too do personal experiences influence the perspective of the author. The personal experiences contribute to the creation of an individual narrative style that adds depth and complexity. As the current of a river carves out its own path, writers' personal experiences help them to find their literary identity. They infuse their work with an individuality that makes it stand apart.

You will find that the flow of your own experiences can be used as a source of stories to share. You can enrich your writing by exploring your memories. By creating a place where self-reflection and vulnerability meet, you can touch readers' hearts with your powerful personal story.

By embracing your personal journey as a source of writing, you are recognizing the intrinsic value in it. In the flow of life, there are many stories and viewpoints that can be explored. You can give your unique experiences a voice by tapping into the flowing flow of life. This will allow you to weave them into stories that are deeply resonant with readers.

Writing about personal experiences is like diving into an ever-flowing river of emotions, memories and moments. You can let them blend together and shape your writing with a fluidity that will immerse you. Personal experiences are like the currents in a river, which ebbs and flows. They offer writers an unlimited source of inspiration.

Imagine yourself stepping in the river and feeling its gentle currents guide you along a journey of transformation. This continuous stream of flowing water represents the reservoirs of experiences that writers can draw from. The richness of the tapestry is in its moments, feelings, and connections. These all intertwine to form their own unique stories.

In the fluidity and honesty of their personal stories, writers can find inspiration. These experiences, like tributaries merging with the main current create a story that is resonant of truth and authenticity. The writers immerse their writing in their personal joys and sorrows. They also include intimate details and authentic emotions that give life to their stories. Their writing is infused with the currents of their personal experience, which shapes their voice and gives it a deep sense of relatability.

You will be amazed at the transformational power that the flow of your personal experience can bring. This flow allows writers to reflect on their journeys, and learn more about themselves and others. In this process, universal themes are revealed as the personal stories illuminate aspects of human life that we all share. Personal experiences become a conduit for empathy and connection, which allows readers to find comfort, inspiration and understanding in the words of the author.

Personal experiences can shape a writer's style and perspective, just as a river shapes its course through the landscape. Their experiences shape the narrative voice of the writer, and infuse it with emotions, personal insights, or revelations. Personal experiences, like the constantly shifting river currents that shape writers' writing, guide them toward an individual literary voice. They give their stories authenticity and capture the essence of what they have experienced.

You will find a wealth of stories waiting to be told in the rhythmic flow of your personal experience. This current can be a great source of inspiration for writers, encouraging them to release memories and feelings onto the paper. This fluidity is where writers can unlock their creativity, as they weave together strands from personal experience to create stories that inspire and resonate with readers.

By using your personal experience as a writing topic, you are embracing the entirety of your journey. This is about recognizing the power and value of your own unique stories and inviting them to be expressed through your writing and to touch other people's hearts. You can tap into an infinite source of inspiration by diving into the river of your personal experience. This will help you create narratives that are effortless and connect with readers.

Writing about personal experiences is similar to immersing oneself in a river of emotions, memories and reflections. The boundaries between the past and present are blurred and the words flow effortlessly into a fluid, seamless narrative. Personal experiences can be a source of constant inspiration for writers, just as a river flows through different landscapes.

Imagine yourself stepping in the river and feeling its currents guide your every move. Water flows swiftly and steadily, reflecting time and personal experience. The continuous stream of water represents your life's tapestry, full of moments of happiness, sorrow, joy and growth. These currents are where writers can find their raw materials for stories, allowing them to shape their words in an authentic, intimate way.

In the fluidity and fluidity of their personal experiences, authors discover an abundance of memories, emotions, and connections. These experiences, like tributaries that merge into the main stream, converge and intertwine into a seamless narrative. The writers use vivid descriptions and emotions to paint their stories. This resonates with the readers at a deep level. Their writing is infused with the currents of their personal experience, which gives it a fluidity and enthralling quality that allows readers to be immersed in the flow of human life.

You will be amazed at the power of transformation that comes from surrendering to your own personal experience. This flow of reflection allows writers to explore the depths and meanings of their journeys. In this process of exploration, universal truths are revealed as the personal stories illuminate aspects that we all share. As readers recognize themselves in the words of a writer, they feel a connection and empathy.

Personal experiences, like the path of a river through a landscape, shape the perspective and the voice of the writer. Their personal experiences shape their stories, giving them a unique style of storytelling. Personal experiences, like the constantly changing river currents that guide writers to their literary identities, give their works an authenticity and a resonance with readers.

Personal experiences become the fluid artistic current which shapes the voice of the writer and makes them stand out.

You can unlock an endless reservoir of stories by using the rhythmic flow of your personal experience as writing material. Writers can dip their pens in the current and allow their emotions and memories to flow on the page. This fluidity allows writers to tap into their creativity, creating narratives which seamlessly combine past and present. Readers are transported into the depths their own personal journeys.

Accepting your personal life experiences to write about is the same as accepting yourself in all of its fullness. This is an acknowledgement of your stories' profound worth, and it allows them to freely flow through your writing. You can tap into a vast source of inspiration by diving into your personal stories. This will help you create narratives with graceful fluidity that connect deeply with the reader and leave a lasting impression on their minds and hearts.

Immerse yourself into the flow of your own personal experience. Let the flow of your thoughts carry you, while you embrace the fluidity and memories. As you begin a journey of transformation, let the flow of life experiences inspire your stories.

Tapping into the Power of Observation

To tap into the power and potential of observation, it is like immersing yourself in a river of continuous perception where each detail, nuance, or thought becomes an ebb in the flow of creative inspiration. As if a river flows through different landscapes, observation helps writers navigate with greater awareness. They can capture moments, emotions and subtleties that give their writing a more fluid, immersive quality.

Imagine yourself standing at the edge of the river, watching the gentle flow of water reflecting everything around you. You step into the currents of the river and your senses are opened to the wide panorama. The continuous flow of the river represents a wellspring for observation. It invites you to be present in the moment and to see the world as it is.

In the fluidity and variety of observations, writers find a treasure trove of inspiration. These observations merge into one another, creating a rich mosaic that enhances their writing. The writers train their senses, eyes and ears to be able to detect the subtlest details, such as the play of lights, cadence in voices or the smallest of gestures, then capture these with words. Their writing is infused with vivid images and an authentic sense of reality when they use the current of observation.

You will be amazed at the power of transformation that comes from surrendering to the flow. This flow allows writers to explore the deepest parts of human experience. The ordinary can become extraordinary when writers discover hidden stories and layers. Observation illuminates our world and opens new paths of connection.

Observation shapes the voice and perspective of the writer, just as the river carves a path in the landscape. This helps them to go beyond the surface and see the true essence of an event or character. They can then convey this with fluidity. As writers draw on their rich observations, they are guided towards authenticity.

The writers find endless inspiration in the rhythmic, continuous flow of observation used as a tool for creativity. This current of inspiration becomes an endless source of new ideas and a continuous flow of sensory information that feeds the imagination. By observing closely, they capture subtleties in human interaction, the nuance of nature and the complex dance of emotion. The beauty of nature and the complexity of human interactions are captured by writers who translate their observations in words to transport the reader into the present moment.

By embracing the power of observation, you are embracing the world as the playground for writers. To see past the surface, to delve deeper into every moment, and to develop a sharp eye for details is to go beyond. Writers can tap into an endless source of inspiration by immersing themselves within the river of observation. They create narratives with vivid fluidity.

To tap into the power and potential of observation, it's like diving in a river where awareness, insight, and currents merge seamlessly, giving your writing a fluid, immersive depth. As the waters of a river cascade together, so too can observation help writers navigate with greater sensitivity. They are able to capture moments, feelings, and specific details, which infuse the work with an engaging fluidity.

Imagine yourself immersed in the ever-changing current of a river. The continuous flow of the river represents observation. It invites you to observe the world, see it, feel it, and take in its essence. Every observation is a ripple. It's an interconnected string that seamlessly weaves into your writing.

In the flow of their observations, writers begin a voyage of discovery. These observations, like tributaries merging into the main stream, form a mosaic that shapes and enriches their writing. The writers sharpen their perceptions by tuning their ears, eyes and hearts to subtleties which are often overlooked. The world is communicated through them, as they translate their observations in words that dance on the page. Their writing is infused with vivid imagery, a sense of intimacy and the current of their observations.

You will witness the transformative powers of this current as you give in to it. As you embrace life with greater awareness, the flow opens up a portal to a deeper understanding. In this world of observation, ordinary things reveal their extraordinary sides. The current reveals the hidden beauty in everyday life, uncovers layers of human interaction, and reveals the deep truths hidden within. The writers use observation to explore the subtleties of human experience, and then convey these with a fluid fluidity.

Observation shapes the voice and perspective of the writer, just as the river shapes its course through the landscape. This helps them to see beyond the surface and delve deeper into a character's or scene's essence, in order to communicate it through a smooth flow of language. This current of observation guides the writer to authenticity and resonance. It allows them to create narratives that take readers right into the middle of the story.

Writers can tap an endless source of creativity by using the rhythmic, continuous flow of observation. This current is a source of inspiration, providing a steady stream of stimuli that feeds imagination. By observing closely, writers can capture nuanced aspects of nature and the play of light and shade, as well as the expressions and gestures of people. The writers become conduits, transforming their observations in words to transport the reader into their stories.

By embracing the power of observing, you embrace a sensory world. Immersing yourself in a river of perceptual flow, being present and open to all the experiences that unfold around you is what it means to embrace the power of observation. You can tap into an endless source of creativity by immersing yourself in this constant stream.

To tap into the power and potential of observation, it's like diving in a river where awareness and insights blend together seamlessly. This gives your writing a fluid, immersive quality. As the waters of a river cascade together, so too can observation help writers navigate with greater sensitivity. They are able to capture moments, feelings, and specific details, which infuse the work with an engaging fluidity.

Imagine yourself immersed in the gentle current of the river, allowing it to guide your movement. This continuous stream of water represents a wellspring that is endless in its observation. It invites you to engage your senses with the world. The world is rich with experiences that are waiting to be translated and explored.

In the flow of their observations, writers are on an ongoing journey of discovery. Each observation, like tributaries merging and intertwining, creates a seamless stream of sensory impressions to enrich the writer's writing. The writers sharpen their perceptions by focusing their attention on subtleties, which are often overlooked. The writers become keen observers who capture the beauty of life, human interactions, and vivid textures. Their writing is infused with vibrant imagery, and a connection between them and the reader.

You will be amazed at the power of transformation that you experience as you give in to this current. This lens opens a new door to understanding the world, and reveals profound truths. It reveals the hidden beauty in the everyday, revealing the moments of extraordinary significance that are often overlooked. The delicate interaction of emotions and the brushstrokes that make up human experience are revealed. The observation becomes a channel for empathy and connections, which allows writers to capture subtleties in the human condition with grace and fluidity.

Observation shapes the voice and perspective of the writer, just as the river traces its course through the landscape. This helps them to see beyond the surface and understand the true essence of characters, scenes, or emotions, then convey that with seamless words. This current of observation guides the writer to authenticity and resonance. It allows them to create narratives that take readers right into the middle of the story.

Writers can tap an endless source of creativity by using the rhythmic, continuous flow of observation. This current is a source of inspiration, providing a steady stream of stimuli that feeds imagination. By observing closely, writers can capture nature's ephemeral splendor, its intricate dance between light and shade, or the fleeting human expressions. The writers become vessels that hold the vibrant tapestry of the world, transforming their observations into words which transport the reader into their stories.

By embracing the power of observation, you immerse yourself in a sensory world. Surrendering to the river of perception is being fully present, receptive and open to all the experiences that unfold around you. You can tap into an endless source of creativity by diving into the continuous flow. Your writing will be infused with grace and beauty.

Surrender to this flowing current of observation. Allow its currents to guide you, allowing your ears, eyes and heart open up. Capture the vivid moments, emotions and details with your writing. Let the river of observations take you on an enlightening journey as you use its power to create narratives which resonate and captivate readers.

**Using Prompts and Exercises to Spark Creativity**

It's like being immersed in a river of creativity, where imagination and inspiration merge to propel your journey of creative exploration with dynamic energy. Prompts and exercises are like the ebbs and flows of the water in a river. They provide constant stimulation that ignites the creativity of your mind and guides it with an effortless and natural flow.

Imagine yourself standing at the edge of the river, watching the shimmering water. You step into the currents and are invited to discover the depths your imagination. The continuous stream of exercises and prompts is the reservoir that awaits you to unlock your creative potential and open up new worlds.

Writers embark on an exciting journey of exploration through the use of fluid prompts and creative exercises. These creative exercises and prompts converge like tributaries into the main stream, creating a tapestry full of possibilities and ideas. These exercises and prompts become the stepping-stones that help you bridge between creativity and inspiration. They provide structure and guidance while still allowing for your imagination to run free.

Your creative process will be infused with dynamic energy by the current of exercises and prompts.

You will be amazed at the power of their transformation as you allow yourself to surrender and follow through with prompts. These prompts and exercises become portals to new worlds, bringing you fresh perspectives and surprising connections. It becomes an exploration catalyst, pushing your creative boundaries and expanding your artistic vision. Exercises and prompts unlock new stories and ideas. They also infuse your work with an originality and novelty.

Prompts and exercises can help you shape your journey of creativity, just as a river shapes its course through the landscape. These exercises and prompts provide direction and structure, helping to navigate creative blockages and uncertainty. These exercises and prompts serve as guideposts that illuminate the path forward, encouraging you to go beyond your comfort zones. This current of exercises and prompts becomes your compass, guiding you to innovative solutions and new perspectives.

You can tap into a never-ending source of creativity by following the rhythmic, continuous flow of exercises and prompts. This current of energy becomes an endless source of inspiration, fueling your creativity. By engaging in prompts and activities, you can stimulate your brain, allowing it to make new connections, and discover fresh ideas. These prompts and exercises become tools to fuel your creativity, leading your thoughts in a fluid way.

By embracing the potential of prompts, exercises and your creativity you can unleash its limitless power. Immersing yourself in a river of creativity, being open to new perspectives and ideas is what it means to embrace the power of prompts and exercises. You can tap into an endless source of creativity and inspiration by immersing yourself in this constant stream.

It's like being immersed in a river of creativity, where imagination and inspiration merge to propel your journey of creative exploration with dynamic energy. Prompts and exercises are like the ebbs and flows of the water in a river. They provide constant stimulation that ignites the creativity of your mind and guides it with an effortless and natural flow.

Imagine yourself standing at the edge of the river, watching the shimmering water. You step into the currents and are invited to discover the depths your imagination. The continuous stream of exercises and prompts is the reservoir that awaits you to unlock your creative potential and open up new worlds.

Writers embark on an exciting journey of exploration through the prompts and exercise. You are carried along by the currents of a river, which gently nudges you to explore unexplored territory in your creative mind. The prompts and exercises become stepping stones, encouraging you to let your imagination wander. The exercises and prompts blend seamlessly as you move through the flow.

You will be amazed at their power to transform you as you allow them to flow through you. The waves become gentle, stirring your imagination and bringing new ideas up to the surface. It becomes an exploration catalyst, pushing you to explore beyond your comfort zone. You dive into the currents of the river with each prompt to discover hidden depths within your creative reservoir.

Prompts and exercises can help you to shape your journey of creativity, just as a river shapes its landscape. The prompts and exercises act as gentle currents to guide your creativity. They encourage you explore new angles, styles and perspectives while the exercises push you to refine and improve your skills. The exercises become a rhythm for your creative process. They guide you towards new insights, and empower you to overcome blocks.

You can tap into an endless source of creativity by following the rhythmic flow of exercises and prompts. Your imagination becomes the river of inspiration. The prompts or exercises blend seamlessly into each other, creating an ever-changing tapestry. As you flow with the inspirations, your journey becomes more creative.

By embracing the creative potential within yourself, you can unleash the full power of the prompts and activities. Immersing yourself in a river of inspiration is a way to embrace its flow, surrender to it, and let the currents carry you to new horizons. You can unlock your imagination by diving into the continuous flow of inspiration. This allows you to embrace the fluidity and creativity of the ideas.

Prompts and exercises can be used to ignite creativity. It's like diving into an endless, fluid river where imagination and currents merge seamlessly, propelled by a dynamic, fluid energy. Like the cascading waters of a river, prompts offer constant stimulation that ignites creativity.

Imagine yourself immersed in the current of a river, and feeling it gently embrace you as it moves forward. This continuous stream of flowing water is a rich source of exercises and prompts, inviting you into a world of endless possibilities. Every prompt or exercise is transformed into a swirling current that guides your exploration of creativity and invites your ideas to flow with the current.

The fluidity and variety of exercises will take writers on an exciting journey. You will be guided through an array of different creative paths by the river, which becomes your inspiration. The prompts and exercise blend together seamlessly like tributaries into the main stream, creating a tapestry that is ever changing. These prompts and exercises become stepping-stones, inspiring you to explore uncharted territory of your imagination.

You will be amazed at the power of their transformation as you allow them to flow through you. These currents become inspiration, stimulating the mind and igniting creativity. It becomes an exploration catalyst, leading you deeper into your own thoughts and uncovering unexplored depths. The prompts and exercises serve as springboards, propelling you imagination in a smooth and unbroken flow.

Prompts and exercises can shape your journey of creativity, just as a river shapes its course through a landscape. These prompts provide direction and structure, which helps you to navigate the ups and downs of your creative process. You are gently guided by the prompts to explore new concepts, expanding your creativity and focusing your attention. Exercises become gentle practice currents that refine your skills while encouraging experimentation. They create a rhythmic flow that propels your creativity in an organic, seamless way.

You can tap into an infinite well of creativity by following the rhythmic flow of exercises and prompts. It is a continuous source of inspiration, feeding your creativity with new ideas and viewpoints. The prompts and exercise merge as you go with the flow. The waves of inspiration carry you effortlessly along, with each new idea moving into the next.

By embracing the prompts and exercises, you are surrendering to inspiration's ever-flowing stream. Immersing yourself in the current and letting its gentle power guide your thoughts is what it means to embrace its inspiration. You can unlock your imagination by diving into the continuous flow. This allows you to embrace the fluidity and creativity of the ideas.

Immerse yourself into the flow of exercises and prompts. Allow the flow of inspiration to guide you, helping your creativity and opening up new ideas. As each exercise and prompt seamlessly merges with the next one, you will be propelled forward in your creative journey. Let the flow of exercises and prompts take you on an inspiring journey as you use their creative power to unlock your imagination, discover new artistic possibilities, and create your most captivating and innovative creations.

Chapter 3: Creating Memorable Characters

Building Multidimensional Characters

It's like creating a river, which is a constant flow of personality and complexity, with each nuance and layer blending seamlessly to create characters that have depth and authenticity. Character development is similar to the way a river navigates through different landscapes. It involves understanding the subtleties of the human mind and allowing emotions, motives and experiences all to come together in a captivating and dynamic flow.

Imagine yourself standing on the banks of a river where water is flowing with an enchanting fluidity. You can explore character depths as you dive into the currents. The endless possibilities of this continuous stream are brought to life by the multidimensionality of characters. The characters are a blend of histories, traits and aspirations that flow seamlessly between them.

In the midst of fluid character development, authors embark on an exciting journey of discovery. Each element in a character merges into the main stream, creating a mosaic that combines personality, beliefs and strengths. The writers delve deep into their characters' minds and hearts to create individuals that breathe and change within the narrative. Character development is the heart of their stories, giving them a sense of authenticity and humanity.

You will be amazed at the power of the character-development current as you allow it to flow through you. As writers become immersed in their characters' lives, the flow opens up a window to empathy. Characters become complex, multi-dimensional beings through the development of their inner contradictions and conflicts. Character development exposes the layers to their personality, revealing their fears, aspirations, pasts and desires. This becomes a way to connect with the reader on an emotional and deep level.

Character development is like a river carving its way through the landscape. It shapes both the story and the impact. Character development shapes the actions and reactions of characters and allows them to move through the narrative with authenticity. Character development is the current that leads writers to create characters who are relatable and invite readers on an emotional adventure with them.

Writers can find endless inspiration in the rhythmic, continuous development of characters. This current is a source of inspiration, an exploration of the human condition. The writers weave the background, experiences, relationships and beliefs of their characters together, so that they can respond and evolve to the conflicts and challenges of the story. The richness and complexity of the characters is enhanced by each layer, resulting in a smooth flow of transformation.

To embrace the complex nature of the human experience is to accept the multidimensionality of the character. Immersing yourself in a river of character creation, exploring their depths and nuances is what it means to embrace the complexity of human existence. You can create characters that resonate with your readers and evoke empathy, understanding and leave a permanent imprint in the narrative.

It's like creating a river that flows with personalities, complexity, and layers. Each layer, nuance, and character is shaped to have depth and authenticity. Character development is like a river that meanders across diverse landscapes. It involves exploring the complexities of human nature and allowing emotions, motivations and experiences to merge and create an engaging flow.

Imagine yourself standing on the banks of a river where water is flowing with an enchanting fluidity. You can explore character depths as you dive into the currents. The endless possibilities of this continuous stream are brought to life by the multidimensionality of characters. The characters are a blend of histories, traits and aspirations that flow seamlessly between them.

In the fluidity that character development provides, writers begin a voyage of discovery. You are carried along the river's currents as it gently guides you in creating complex, compelling characters. Each element in a character merges into the main stream, creating a mosaic that combines personality, values, flaws and strengths. In this convergence, characters take on a new level of authenticity and depth. They become more than just figments.

You will be amazed at the power of the character-development current as you allow it to flow through you. As writers become immersed in their character's lives, the flow can lead to empathy. Characters transcend the pages of a book by embracing the contradictions and complexities that are inherently human. Character development reveals the facets of each character, including their fears, aspirations, pasts and desires. This becomes a way to connect with readers and understand the human condition.

Character development is like a river carving its way through the landscape. It shapes both the story and the impact. Character development shapes the actions and reactions of characters and allows them to move through the narrative with authenticity. Character development is the current that leads writers to create characters who are relatable and invite readers on a journey with them.

Writers can find endless inspiration in the rhythmic, continuous development of characters. This current is a source of inspiration, an exploration of the human condition. The writers weave the background, experiences, and beliefs of their characters together, so that they can respond and evolve to the conflicts and challenges of the story. The richness and complexity of the characters is enhanced by each layer, resulting in a smooth flow of transformation.

To embrace the complex nature of the human experience is to accept the multidimensionality of the character. Immersing yourself in the river of character creation, exploring their depths and intricacies is what it means to embrace the complexity of human existence. You can create characters that resonate with your readers and evoke empathy, understanding and leave a permanent imprint in the narrative.

It's like slipping along the river of imagination. Each twist and turn brings out new depths. Character development is similar to the way that river waters merge seamlessly. It involves weaving together traits, feelings, and experiences in order to create individuals with authenticity and depth. Character building is a current that carries you along on your journey of creativity with an interconnected and fluid energy.

Imagine yourself stepping in the embrace of the river, letting its soft current caress you. The flowing river represents the infinite possibilities of the world, with its multi-dimensional characters. The character is a harmonious mosaic, blending facets in harmony.

Writers embark on an exciting exploration of the character's fluidity. You are carried along by the river, which gently nudges you towards your character's identity. Each element in a character merges seamlessly, adding to its uniqueness. This current is a catalyst that swirls with their motivations and personalities to create multidimensional characters who breathe and develop within the story.

You will be amazed at the power of character creation as you allow it to flow through you. This allows you to feel empathy for your characters and immerse yourself into their lives. They become three-dimensional characters with layers of meaning that appear like the meandering river. It reveals their thoughts and emotions in all their complexity, inviting the reader to experience their human side on a deeper level.

Character development is like a river carving its path through the landscape. It shapes the plot and the impact of the story. Character development affects how characters react and perceive their environment, creating an authentic and dynamic flow. Character building is a current that guides writers in creating characters who are able to resonate with their readers. They can evoke genuine emotions and create lasting connections.

The continuous flow of character creation provides writers with an infinite source of inspiration. It is the current of the river that provides a continuous stream of inspiration, allowing writers to explore human nature. The writers immerse themselves in the complexities of characters, their relationships and their experiences. They navigate through their currents. The layers merge seamlessly, adding nuance and depth, creating an engaging flow of transformation and growth.

To embrace the complexity of the human experience is to accept the challenge of creating multi-dimensional characters. Surrendering to character development and letting its current guide you is what it means to explore. You can create characters that feel real, with the burden of their memories and dreams for the future. The river of character growth carries readers on an enlightening journey.

Immerse yourself into the flow of character growth. Allow the current to guide you as you explore, and allow your characters breathe authentically. Accept the fluidity in their development, as they seamlessly merge into one another, forming individuals that captivate and resonate. The river of character-building will take you on an incredible journey as you use its powerful force to develop multidimensional characters that inspire and provoke.

Crafting Engaging Dialogue

It's like creating a river of continuous conversation where currents merge to create interactions that are captivating and powerful. As the waters of a river ebbs and flows, so does dialogue, giving characters dynamism and energy.

Imagine yourself stepping into a river of dialogue. Feel its currents embrace you and invite you to explore human expression. The art of creating engaging dialogue is a continuous stream of words that flow effortlessly and carry the emotions, intents, and revelations. The dialogue lines become ripples, blending and intertwining to create a natural flow.

In the process of creating engaging dialogues, writers begin a journey in communication. Each character's voices converge like tributaries into the main stream, creating a harmonious symphony with diverse personalities and perspectives. Their thoughts, emotions, and desires are reflected in the river, which shapes conversations and reveals the deepest depths of the relationships.

You will be amazed at the power of dialogue as you allow it to flow through you. The dialogue becomes a link between characters and the reader, inviting the latter into the story. As dialogue mimics real life conversation, the flow of the story becomes authentic. Characters come alive through engaging dialogue. They express their fears, hopes and conflicts on an emotional level.

As the river traces its course through the landscape so does engaging dialogue shape the trajectory of the story and the impact it has. The dialogue shapes the dynamic between characters and allows their interaction to be natural. It is the current of dialogue that directs writers to conversations that will reveal the character's depth, move the plot along, create tension or humor and provide revelations.

In the constant, flowing rhythm that comes with crafting engaging dialogues, writers can tap into an infinite source of inspiration. Characters speak authentically and with purpose when the river is a source of expressions and words. The writers explore cadence and tone to ensure that the dialogue is in line with each character's unique personality and motivations. The dialogue flows seamlessly from one line to the next. This creates a compelling and rich flow that engages and invests readers.

To embrace the craft of creating engaging dialogue, is to embrace communication's essence. Immersing yourself in the river of dialogue and allowing it to influence your character's words and feelings is what this means. You can create dialogues that are authentic and resonate by immersing yourself in this constant stream.

It's like gliding along the meandering currents of a river, where communication flows seamlessly and shapes interactions that are captivating. As the waters of a river flow, so does dialogue, giving characters dynamism and energy.

Imagine yourself stepping into a river of dialogue. Feel its gentle currents embrace you and invite you to explore human expression. The art of creating engaging dialogue is a continuous stream of words that flow effortlessly and carry the emotions, intentions, or revelations. The dialogue lines become ripples, as they merge and intertwine with each other, creating an authentic and captivating flow.

Writers embark on an adventure of communication through the fluidity in crafting engaging dialogue. As a channel, the river guides characters' exchanges of ideas and words. Each character's voices converge, like tributaries merging with the main current. This creates a harmonious symphony combining diverse personalities and perspectives. This convergence is where dialogues take shape and reveal the true nature of the relationships.

You will be amazed at the power of dialogue as you allow it to flow through you. The dialogue becomes the bridge between characters and the reader, welcoming them to the core of the story. As dialogue mimics real life conversation, the flow of dialogue becomes authentic. Characters find their voices through engaging dialogue. They express their fears, hopes and conflicts on an emotional level.

As the river channels its way through the landscape to create a narrative, engaging dialogue can also shape the trajectory and impact of the story. The dialogue shapes the dynamic between characters and allows their interaction to be natural. It is the current of dialogue that directs writers to conversations that will reveal the character's depth, move the plot along, create tension or humor and provide revelations.

In the constant, flowing rhythm that comes with crafting engaging dialogues, writers can tap into a never-ending source of inspiration. Characters speak authentically and with purpose when the river is bursting with words and expressions. The writers explore cadence and tone to ensure that the dialogue is in line with each character's unique personality and motivation. The dialogue flows seamlessly from one line to the next. This creates a compelling and rich flow that engages and invests readers.

To embrace the craft of creating engaging dialogue, is to embrace communication's essence. Immersing yourself in the river of dialogue and allowing it to influence your character's words and feelings is what this means. You can create dialogues that are authentic and resonate by immersing yourself in this constant stream.

It's like floating along a river of continuous conversation where currents merge to create interactions that are both captivating and resonant. As the river flows through different landscapes, the dialogue gives characters a life and brings the story to vibrant, fluid, dynamic energy.

Imagine yourself immersed in the gentle flow of the dialogue. It will guide you to the subtleties of expression. The art of creating engaging dialogue is to create a continuous stream of words that flow effortlessly. The lines of dialogue become ripples, which blend and intertwine with each other, creating a captivating and harmonious exchange of words.

In the process of creating engaging dialogue, authors embark on a communication journey. You are carried along the river's currents and invited to discover your character's voices. As tributaries merge into the main stream, characters' unique perspectives and personalities converge to create a symphony. This convergence is where dialogues gain depth and authenticity. They become a powerful storytelling tool.

You will be amazed at the power of engaging dialogue as you allow it to flow through you. The dialogue becomes the bridge between characters and the reader, bringing them to the core of the story. As dialogue mimics real life conversation, it becomes an avenue for understanding. Characters reveal their emotions and thoughts through engaging dialogue. This fosters intimacy with the reader and a feeling of empathy.

As the river shapes its course through the landscape so does engaging dialogue shape the trajectory of the story and the impact it has. The dialogue influences the way characters interrelate, illuminates their relationships, and drives plot forward. It acts as a guide, leading writers to conversations that will reveal the character's depth, drive story momentum and trigger powerful emotions.

Writers can tap into an infinite wellspring of creativity by creating engaging dialogue in a continuous and flowing rhythm. It is through the river that characters are brought to life by their own unique voice. The writers navigate through the language and tone of characters to ensure authenticity and consistency. The dialogue flows seamlessly from one line to the next. This creates a captivating and natural flow, which keeps readers engaged.

To embrace the craft of creating engaging dialogue, is to embrace human connection. Immerse yourself into the river of dialogue, and let its currents guide the words and emotions of your characters. You can create dialogues that are dynamic and engaging by immersing yourself in this constant stream. This continuous stream can be used to develop characters, advance plots, and engage readers.

Immerse yourself into the flow of creating engaging dialogue. Explore character interaction by letting the current lead you. Capture their intentions, thoughts and conflicts. Allow your character's voices to be authentic and fluid. Allow the dialogue to take you on an exciting journey as you use its powerful power to craft conversations that will captivate and resonate with your audience.

Developing Character Arcs and Motivations

Character arcs, motivations, and growth are like the flow of a river, as currents merge to create characters with authenticity and depth. Character development is like guiding people on a self-discovery journey, where their inner journeys and motivations converge to create an exciting and dynamic flow.

Imagine yourself stepping into a river of motivations and character arcs. Feel its currents embracing you as you explore the depths human transformation. The realm of possibility is represented by this continuous and flowing stream. The character is a blend of fears, desires and aspirations that flows seamlessly through each stage.

The fluidity in character motivations and arcs takes writers on an evolutionary journey. They are guided along currents of growth by the river. Each element of the character's story converges like tributaries into the main stream, creating a rich tapestry that reflects personal transformation and growth. This flow is a powerful catalyst that helps characters evolve.

You will be amazed at the power of transformation that occurs when you allow the character motivations to flow through you. The flow becomes a reflection of the human condition, inviting the reader to engage with characters at a deep and emotional level. As characters face new challenges and struggle with inner conflict, the flow of the story becomes an avenue for understanding. Characters that are well developed and have strong motivations can transcend fiction and resonate with readers.

Character arcs, motivations and the trajectory of the story are shaped by them in the same way that a river carves a path across the landscape. Character arcs and motivations shape the perceptions and actions of characters and allow them to move through the narrative with authenticity. Character development is the current that helps writers create arcs which reveal character growth, question belief systems and explore human emotions.

Writers can find endless inspiration in the flowing, continuous rhythms of character motivations and arcs. Characters undergo significant changes as a result of their desires and motivations. The river is a source of endless possibilities. The writers delve deep into their character's past, beliefs and experiences to allow them to respond and evolve to challenges and conflict in the story.

The character's story is woven together seamlessly, so that the flow of change feels natural.

By embracing the complex human experience, you can embrace character motivations and arcs. Immersing yourself in the river of purpose and growth, you can allow its currents guide your character's journey. You can create characters who resonate with your readers and undergo transformations which evoke empathy.

Character arcs, motivations, and growth are like a river that flows continuously, morphing and changing, forming characters with authenticity and depth. Character development is similar to the journey that a river takes through different landscapes. It involves taking individuals on an inner journey, where their motives and stories converge, creating a captivating and dynamic flow.

Imagine yourself immersed in the gentle currents that flow through character motivations and arcs. They will guide you to the intricacies in human transformation. The realm of possibility is represented by this continuous and flowing stream. The character is a blend of fears, desires and aspirations that flows seamlessly through each stage.

The fluidity in character motivations and arcs takes writers on a growth-and-evolution journey. They are guided along currents of transformation by the river. Each element of the character's story converges like tributaries into the main stream, creating a rich tapestry that reflects personal growth. This flow is a catalyst to self-realization and helps create characters who evolve within the story.

You will be amazed at the power of transformation that occurs when you allow the character motivations to flow through you. The flow becomes a reflection of the human condition, inviting the reader to engage with characters at a deep and emotional level. As characters face their fears and desires, the flow of the story becomes an avenue to understanding. Characters with well-developed motivations and character arcs transcend fiction boundaries, and leave a lasting impression on the hearts and minds of readers.

Character arcs, like the path of a river through a landscape, shape the story's trajectory. Characters are shaped by their perceptions, behaviors, and transformations. This allows them to believably and authentically navigate through the narrative currents. Character development is the current that helps writers create arcs which reveal character growth, question belief systems and explore human emotions.

Writers can find endless inspiration in the flowing, continuous rhythms of character motivations and arcs. Characters undergo significant changes as a result of their desires and motivations. The river is a source of endless possibilities. The writers delve deep into their character's past, beliefs and experiences to allow them to respond and evolve to challenges and conflict in the story. The character's story is woven together seamlessly, creating an engaging flow.

By embracing the complex human experience, you can embrace character motivations and arcs. Immerse yourself into the river of purpose and growth, and let its currents guide your character's journey. You can create characters who resonate with your readers and undergo transformations which evoke empathy.

Character arcs, motivations, and the journey of self-discovery are like a river that flows continuously, transforming characters into people with authenticity and depth. Character development is like guiding people on a self-discovery journey, where their inner stories and motivations converge to create an engaging flow.

Imagine yourself floating down the gentle river current of motivations and character arcs. It will carry you along through all the complexities of the human transformation. The flowing river represents the world of infinite possibilities, where characters are brought to life. The characters are a blend of fears, desires and aspirations. They seamlessly transition from one development stage to another.

The fluidity and motivations of characters and plots take writers on an evolutionary journey. It is the river that guides them through their journey of transformation. The currents gently guide them. Each element of the character's story converges like tributaries into the main stream, resulting in a tapestry rich with personal growth. The flow is a powerful catalyst that propels characters on their journey, forming their values and beliefs within the story.

You will be amazed at the power of transformation that occurs when you allow the character motivations to flow through you. The flow becomes a reflection of the human condition, allowing readers to relate on an emotional and profound level. As characters go on quests within, face their fears and follow their dreams, the flow opens up a portal to understanding. Characters that are well-crafted and have strong motivations leave a lasting impression on the reader's heart and mind.

Character arcs, like the course of a river through a landscape, shape the story's trajectory. The characters are shaped by their perceptions, behaviors, and changes, which allows them to move through the narrative with authenticity. Character development is the current that guides the writers to create arcs which reveal character growth, question belief systems and explore human emotions.

Writers can find endless inspiration in the flowing, continuous rhythms of character motivations and arcs. Characters undergo significant changes as a result of their desires and motivations. The river is a source of endless possibilities. The writers delve deep into their character's past, beliefs and experiences to allow them to respond and evolve to challenges and conflict in the story. The character's story is woven together seamlessly, creating an engaging flow.

To embrace the complexity of human life, you must be willing to develop character motivations and arcs. Immersing yourself in the river of purpose and growth, you can allow its currents guide your character's journey. You can create characters who resonate with your readers and undergo transformations which evoke empathy.

Surrender yourself to this flowing current of motivations and character arcs. Allow its flow to guide you as you explore your personal growth and challenges. Allow your character's motivations and their journeys to naturally flow, so that they reflect the complexity of human experience. Allow the river of character growth to take you on an exciting journey as you use its strength to develop multidimensional characters that will captivate and inspire your readers, while leaving a lasting impression on your story.

Chapter 4: Constructing Compelling Plots

Understanding Story Structure

Story structure can be compared to a river, a seamless, continuous narrative where plot, tension and resolution are seamlessly merged, creating a cohesive and compelling storytelling experience. Story structure is like a river that navigates across different landscapes. It provides the framework for events to flow, creating an engaging and dynamic journey.

Imagine yourself immersed in a river, allowing its gentle currents to carry you along the intricate details of storytelling. The architecture of the narrative is represented by this flowing river, in which the elements of rising action, climaxes, falling actions, and resolution are all harmoniously blended to form a cohesive and compelling flow.

The fluidity of the story's structure is a journey of creation for writers. It becomes their imagination and ideas' guide through plot twists and turn. Each plot, conflict and revelation merges into the main stream, like tributaries. This creates a narrative flow that is well-paced. This stream acts as a guide for writers to organize their stories and maintain readers' interest.

You will be amazed at the strength of a coherent narrative when you allow the story to flow. As events progress and build to climactic points, the flow becomes a vehicle for tension and excitement. As readers follow along and eagerly anticipate resolution, the flow creates emotional investment. By using a carefully crafted structure for their stories, authors can ensure that they are engaging and impactful to readers.

Story structure is like a river carving its way through the landscape. It determines how the story will unfold. The story structure is the basis for character growth, conflict intensification, and theme exploration. Story structure is the driving force that ensures events are logical and believable, and keeps readers invested and engaged.

The rhythmic flow of a story allows writers to create their stories with ease. It becomes an inspiration source where authors can try out different narratives and plots. This allows writers to seamlessly integrate character development, conflict and resolution.

Understanding story structure means embracing the art of telling stories. Immersing yourself in the river of story, and allowing the currents to shape your dramatic arc is what it means to embrace the art of storytelling. You can create compelling narratives by immersing yourself in this constant stream.

Story structure can be compared to a river, a seamless, continuous narrative where plot, tension and resolution all flow together seamlessly, creating a cohesive and compelling storytelling experience. Story structure is like a river that meanders across diverse landscapes. It provides the framework for events to flow, which creates a dynamic journey.

Imagine yourself immersed in the flow of a story, and letting its gentle currents carry you along the intricate details of telling a tale. The architecture of the narrative is represented by this flowing river, in which the elements of rising action, climaxes, falling actions, and resolution are all harmoniously blended to form a cohesive and compelling flow.

The fluidity of the story's structure is a journey of creation for writers. It becomes their imagination and ideas' guide through plot twists and turn. Each plot, conflict and revelation merges into the main stream, like tributaries. This creates a well-paced, engaging narrative. This stream acts as a guide for writers to organize their stories and maintain readers' interest.

You will be amazed at the strength of a coherent narrative when you allow the story to flow. As events progress and climactic scenes are reached, the flow becomes a vehicle for tension and excitement. As readers follow along and eagerly anticipate resolution, the flow creates emotional investment. By using a carefully crafted structure for their stories, authors can ensure that they are engaging and impactful to readers.

Story structure is like a river carving its way through the landscape. It determines how the story will unfold. The story structure is the basis for character growth, conflict intensification, and theme exploration. Story structure is the driving force that ensures events are logical and purposeful, and keeps readers invested and engaged.

The rhythmic flow of a story allows writers to create their stories with ease. It becomes an inspiration source where authors can try out different narratives and plots. This allows for seamless character development, conflict and resolution to be seamlessly integrated, resulting in a rewarding and immersive reading experience.

Understanding story structure means embracing the art of telling stories. Immerse yourself into the river of story, and let its currents guide the plot progression. You can create compelling narratives by immersing yourself in this constant stream.

Story structure can be compared to gliding down a river, where plot, tension and resolution all merge together seamlessly. This creates a captivating and immersive story-telling experience. Story structure is like a river that navigates across different landscapes. It provides the framework for events to flow, and creates a dynamic journey.

Imagine yourself immersed in the gentle flow of the story structure. Its currents will guide you to the depths of the art of storytelling. The flowing river represents the narrative blueprint, in which the elements of rising action, climaxes, falling actions, and resolution are all blended together to form a coherent and compelling flow.

The fluidity of the story structure is a journey of creativity for writers. It is the river that guides their imagination and ideas through plot twists and turn. Each plot, conflict and revelation merges into a well-paced narrative. This stream acts as a guide for writers to organize the events in a way that keeps readers interested.

You will be amazed at the power of structure in creating a satisfying and coherent narrative. As the story unfolds, it creates tension as you anticipate the climactic moment. As readers follow along eagerly to discover the conclusion and closure, they become emotionally engaged. By using a carefully crafted structure for their stories, authors can ensure that they have an impact on readers and make them feel something.

Story structure is like a river carving its way through the landscape. It determines how the story will unfold. The story structure provides the foundation for character growth, conflict intensification, and theme exploration. Story structure is the driving force that ensures events are logical and purposeful, and keeps readers invested and engaged.

The continuous flow of story structure provides writers with an infinite source of inspiration. It becomes an endless source of inspiration, allowing writers to experiment with plots and subplots. The river allows seamless integration of different story elements to create a coherent and immersive reading experience.

Understanding story structure means embracing the art of telling stories. You must surrender to the river currents of the narrative and allow them to shape your dramatic arc. You can create dynamic narratives by diving into the continuous flow.

Let the flow of your story guide you. Allow its flow to guide you as you explore plot, tension and resolution. Allow your narrative to be fluid, and let the elements of your story flow. This will take readers on an exciting journey. Allow the story's structure to take you on an adventure as you use its strength to craft narratives that will captivate and inspire your readers.

Incorporating Conflict and Tension

Incorporating conflict and tension into a story is similar to weaving a continuous, flowing stream of dramatic energy in which the currents of struggle and anticipation blend smoothly, producing a dynamic and compelling storytelling experience. Conflict and tension form the course of a narrative, providing complexity and fascination to the people and their travels, just as the river carves its route across varied landscapes.

Imagine yourself immersed in a river of conflict and tension, feeling the currents spark emotions and force the tale along. This rushing river symbolizes the center of dramatic storytelling, when opposing forces collide, challenges occur, and stakes are heightened. Each conflict ripple blends seamlessly into the next, creating a sense of anticipation and propelling the story with an unstoppable flow.

Writers start on a journey of storytelling skill within the fluidity of infusing conflict and tension. The river serves as a conduit for the characters' conflicting wants, beliefs, and goals, guiding them through trials and tribulations. Each conflict point and moment of tension combines, producing a gripping and intentional narrative flow, much like tributaries merging into the main river. The stream acts as a compass, leading writers to carefully place barriers, problems, and periods of doubt in order to keep readers interested.

You observe the transformational power of the conflict and tension current as you succumb to it. It becomes the narrative's heartbeat, infusing it with a feeling of urgency and emotional intensity. As the characters confront their anxieties, face moral quandaries, and fight for their ambitions, the flow serves as a catalyst for character development. Writers guarantee that their novels capture readers and make a lasting impression by incorporating conflict and tension.

Conflict and tension cut the trajectory of the story in the same way that the river carves its route through the landscape. They create the necessary peaks and valleys that shape the mounting action, climax, and resolution. The stream of conflict and tension becomes the driving force, carrying the tale toward its climax and resolution while keeping readers riveted.

Writers tap into a fountain of storytelling possibilities by combining conflict and tension in a continuous, flowing rhythm. The river serves as a source of inspiration for authors, allowing them to explore many causes of conflict, internal and external challenges, and unexpected turns. It enables the seamless blending of tension, excitement, and emotional resonance, resulting in an engaging and immersive reading experience.

Accepting the art of combining conflict and tension is accepting the core of narrative. It is to give in to the ebb and flow of dramatic energy, allowing its currents to steer the conflicts and tensions that define the story. By entering this never-ending stream, you get the ability to construct narratives that are captivating, emotionally charged, and resonate with readers.

Incorporating conflict and tension into a story is similar to navigating a continuous, flowing river of dramatic energy, where the currents of struggle and anticipation mix smoothly, producing a dynamic and fascinating storytelling experience. Conflict and tension create the trajectory of a narrative, infusing it with complexity, interest, and emotional resonance, just as the river carves its route across varied landscapes.

Imagine yourself immersed in a river of conflict and tension, feeling its currents surge and swirl, forcing the tale onward with an unstoppable momentum. The core of narrative is represented by this rushing stream, where opposing forces combine, difficulties occur, and emotions run strong. Each conflict ripple blends into the next, creating a sense of urgency and propelling the narrative forward with unbroken pace.

Writers engage on a creative journey while infusing conflict and tension. The river serves as a conduit for the characters' conflicting wants, beliefs, and goals, guiding them through trials and tribulations. Each conflict point and moment of tension melts into the main river, providing a continuous and fascinating narrative flow. The stream acts as a compass, leading writers to carefully place barriers, problems, and periods of doubt in order to keep readers completely involved.

You observe the transformational power of the conflict and tension current as you succumb to it. It becomes the narrative's lifeblood, pulsing through its veins, boosting emotions and producing a sense of anticipation. As the characters confront their anxieties, encounter moral quandaries, and undergo personal growth, the flow serves as a catalyst for character development. Writers guarantee that their novels capture readers and make a lasting impression by incorporating conflict and tension.

Conflict and tension define the trajectory of the story in the same way as the river carves its route through the landscape. They supply the peaks and troughs, growing action, and climax moments that keep readers interested and invested. The current of conflict and tension becomes the driving force, moving the tale forward and keeping readers on the edge of their seats.

Writers tap into an infinite amount of tale possibilities by combining conflict and tension in a continuous, flowing rhythm. The river becomes a source of inspiration for authors, allowing them to explore all forms of conflicts - internal and external, physical and emotional - and the tensions that occur as a result of them. It enables the seamless blending of suspense, excitement, and emotional resonance, resulting in a tale that captures readers from beginning to end.

Accepting the art of adding conflict and tension is to accept the core of narrative. It is to give in to the ebb and flow of dramatic energy, allowing its currents to steer the conflicts and tensions that define the story. By delving into this never-ending stream, you get the ability to construct narratives that are intriguing, engaging, and genuinely resonate with readers.

Incorporating conflict and suspense into a story is similar to navigating a continuous, flowing river of storytelling, where the currents of struggle and anticipation mix smoothly, producing a dynamic and compelling experience for readers. Conflict and tension determine the direction of a narrative, infusing it with complexity, suspense, and emotional intensity, just as the river runs through varied landscapes.

Imagine yourself immersed in a river of conflict and tension, feeling its currents carry the tale onward with an unstoppable flow. This rushing stream symbolizes the center of narrative, where opposing forces combine, difficulties develop, and emotions run strong. Each dramatic twist and turn mixes well with the next, creating a sense of urgency and propelling the narrative with consistent vigor.

Writers start on a path of narrative mastery within the fluidity of infusing conflict and tension. The river serves as a channel for the conflicting wants, beliefs, and motivations of the characters, guiding them through trials and tribulations. Each conflict point and moment of tension easily blends into the main stream, producing a continuous and interesting narrative flow. The stream acts as a compass, leading writers in carefully putting barriers, conflicts, and periods of doubt in order to keep readers interested.

You observe the transformational power of the conflict and tension current as you succumb to it. It becomes the story's lifeblood, amplifying emotions, propelling character development, and immersing readers in the narrative. As characters experience internal and external difficulties, overcome their anxieties, and strive for their aspirations, the flow becomes a catalyst for progress. Writers guarantee that their narratives capture, resound, and elicit powerful emotional responses by skillfully incorporating conflict and tension.

Conflict and tension define the trajectory of the story in the same way as the river carves its route through the landscape. They supply the peaks and troughs, growing action, and climax moments that keep readers interested and invested. The current of conflict and tension serves as the driving force, forcing the tale forward while keeping readers on the edge of their seats.

Writers tap into an infinite amount of creative potential by combining conflict and tension in a continuous, flowing rhythm. The river becomes a source of inspiration for authors, allowing them to explore many sorts of conflicts - internal and external, interpersonal and intrapersonal - and the tensions that occur as a result of them. It enables the seamless blending of suspense, excitement, and emotional resonance, resulting in a tale that captures readers from start to finish.

Accepting the art of adding conflict and tension is to accept the core of narrative. It is to give in to the ebb and flow of narrative energy, allowing its currents to steer the conflicts and tensions that build the story. By entering this never-ending stream, you get the ability to construct narratives that are intriguing, engaging, and leave a lasting impression on readers.

So, yield to the ebb and flow of absorbing conflict and tension. Allow its current state to direct your investigation of narrative hurdles, confrontations, and uncertainty. Allowing your story's conflicts to flow organically, raising suspense and moving the narrative ahead, embrace the fluidity of building tension and dramatic energy. Allow the river of conflict and tension to lead you on a transforming narrative trip as you harness its potential to fascinate, excite, and leave a lasting impression on your readers.

Utilizing Plot Devices and Twists

Using plot devices and twists is similar to navigating a continuous, flowing river of narrative surprises, where the currents of unexpected turns and ingenious gadgets mix flawlessly to create a dynamic and fascinating storytelling experience. Plot devices and twists influence the direction of a story, filling it with intrigue, tension, and moments of revelation, just as the river runs through varied landscapes.

Imagine immersing yourself in a river of narrative devices and turns, allowing its currents to transport you along the story's unexpected paths. This flowing stream exemplifies the art of surprise and suspense, in which unexpected occurrences, disclosures, and ingenious narrative strategies seamlessly mix, keeping readers intrigued and ready to see what lies around the next curve. Each twist and turn merges smoothly into the narrative, creating a sense of excitement and moving the plot along with an ever-present flow of interest.

Writers start on a voyage of narrative manipulation through the fluidity of deploying story devices and twists. The river serves as a channel for surprising twists, character insights, and brilliant structural decisions. Each plot device and twist converges into the main stream, providing a continuous and engaging narrative flow. The stream transforms into a compass, leading writers in deliberately putting shocks, unexpected connections, and ingenious insights to keep readers guessing.

You experience their transformational force as you submit to the torrent of story devices and twists. They become the seasoning that adds depth, interest, and levels of complexity to the plot. The flow serves as a catalyst for increased tension and reader involvement, as they await the next unexpected turn of events. Writers guarantee that their narratives engage, delight, and astound readers by skillfully utilizing plot elements and twists.

Plot devices and plot twists affect the trajectory of the story in the same way as the river carves its path through the landscape. They supply the unexpected peaks, narrative changes, and "a-ha" moments that keep readers engaged and guessing. The torrent of narrative devices and twists becomes the driving force, moving the novel towards climax discoveries while immersing readers in a never-ending stream of shocks.

Writers draw into a wealth of imagination and originality inside the constant, flowing rhythm of deploying narrative devices and twists. The river becomes a playground for authors to experiment with various methods, such as foreshadowing, dramatic irony, surprising character motives, or creatively arranged timeframes. It enables the seamless blending of shocks, suspense, and reader involvement, resulting in a story that keeps readers on the edge of their seats.

Embracing the art of narrative devices and twists is embracing the core of storytelling surprise. It is to succumb to the raging river of narrative unpredictability, letting its currents to steer the story's shocks and turns. By plunging into this never-ending stream, you have the ability to build tales that are full of surprising twists, smart devices, and moments of discovery that leave readers with a lasting impression.

Using plot devices and twists is like stepping into a never-ending river of narrative surprises, where the currents of unexpected turns and ingenious gadgets blend flawlessly to create a dynamic and fascinating storytelling experience. Plot devices and twists influence the direction of a story, filling it with intrigue, tension, and moments of revelation, just as the river runs through varied landscapes.

Immerse yourself in the river of plot devices and turns, allowing its currents to transport you along the story's unexpected paths. This flowing stream exemplifies the art of surprise and suspense, in which unexpected occurrences, discoveries, and ingenious narrative strategies seamlessly mix, keeping readers captivated and anxiously anticipating what lies around the next curve. Each twist and turn merges smoothly into the narrative, building excitement and moving the plot along with a constant flow of curiosity.

Writers start on a voyage of narrative manipulation through the fluidity of deploying story devices and twists. The river serves as a channel for unexpected aspects, character growth, and story choices. Each plot device and twist converges into the main stream, providing a continuous and engaging narrative flow. The stream takes on the role of a compass, helping writers in deliberately putting shocks, surprising connections, and brilliant insights to keep readers fascinated.

Allow yourself to get carried away by the stream of narrative devices and twists and see their transformational impact. They become the flavoring that adds depth, interest, and levels of complexity to the plot. The flow serves as a catalyst for increased tension and reader involvement, as they await the next unexpected turn of events. Writers guarantee that their narratives engage, delight, and astound readers by skillfully utilizing plot elements and twists.

Plot devices and plot twists affect the trajectory of the story in the same way as the river carves its path through the landscape. They present readers with surprising peaks, narrative changes, and "aha" moments that keep them involved and guessing. The stream of narrative devices and twists becomes the driving force, bringing the drama towards climax discoveries while keeping the surprises flowing.

Writers draw into a wealth of imagination and originality inside the constant, flowing rhythm of deploying narrative devices and twists. The river becomes a playground for authors to experiment with various methods like as foreshadowing, dramatic irony, surprising character motives, and skillfully arranged timeframes. It enables the seamless blending of shocks, suspense, and reader involvement, resulting in a story that keeps readers on the edge of their seats.

Using plot devices and twists is like stepping into a never-ending river of narrative surprises, where the currents of unexpected turns and ingenious gadgets blend flawlessly to create a dynamic and fascinating storytelling experience. Plot devices and twists influence the direction of a story, filling it with intrigue, tension, and moments of revelation, just as the river runs through varied landscapes.

Immerse yourself in the river of plot devices and turns, allowing its currents to transport you along the story's unexpected paths. This flowing stream exemplifies the art of surprise and suspense, in which unexpected occurrences, discoveries, and ingenious narrative strategies seamlessly mix, keeping readers captivated and anxiously anticipating what lies around the next curve. Each twist and turn merges smoothly into the narrative, building excitement and moving the plot along with a constant flow of curiosity.

Writers start on a voyage of narrative manipulation through the fluidity of deploying story devices and twists. The river serves as a channel for unexpected aspects, character growth, and story choices. Each plot device and twist converges into the main stream, providing a continuous and engaging narrative flow. The stream takes on the role of a compass, helping writers in deliberately putting shocks, surprising connections, and brilliant insights to keep readers fascinated.

Allow yourself to get carried away by the stream of narrative devices and twists and see their transformational impact. They become the flavoring that adds depth, interest, and levels of complexity to the plot. The flow serves as a catalyst for increased tension and reader involvement, as they await the next unexpected turn of events. Writers guarantee that their narratives engage, delight, and astound readers by skillfully utilizing plot elements and twists.

Plot devices and plot twists affect the trajectory of the story in the same way as the river carves its path through the landscape. They present readers with surprising peaks, narrative changes, and "aha" moments that keep them involved and guessing. The stream of narrative devices and twists becomes the driving force, bringing the drama towards climax discoveries while keeping the surprises flowing.

Writers draw into a wealth of imagination and originality inside the constant, flowing rhythm of deploying narrative devices and twists. The river becomes a playground for authors to experiment with various methods like as foreshadowing, dramatic irony, surprising character motives, and skillfully arranged timeframes. It enables the seamless blending of shocks, suspense, and reader involvement, resulting in a story that keeps readers on the edge of their seats.

Accept the art of using story devices and twists, and give in to the rushing river of narrative unpredictability. Allow its current state to inspire your discovery of unexpected components, ingenious twists, and stunning findings. Allow your story's narrative to flow naturally while keeping readers interested and anxiously flipping the pages by embracing the flexibility of introducing surprises and inventive methods. Allow the river of plot devices and twists to lead you on a transforming storytelling trip as you harness its ability to fascinate, excite, and leave readers speechless with your narrative prowess.

Chapter 5: Crafting Vivid Settings

Utilizing Sensory Details to Enhance Descriptions

Using sensory details to improve descriptions is like immersing oneself in a never-ending river of vivid sensations, where the currents of sight, sound, smell, taste, and touch blend flawlessly to create a rich and immersive storytelling experience. Sensory nuances build the fabric of a narrative, producing a multi-dimensional image that engages readers' senses and takes them into the world of the tale, much as the river meanders over varied landscapes.

Consider delving into a river of sensory details and letting its currents lead you on a trip of bright sensations. This rushing stream depicts the palette of storytelling, where colors, sounds, scents, sensations, and textures merge together to bring the story to life. Each sensory detail blends into the next, resulting in a constant flow of feelings that capture readers' imaginations.

Writers engage on a mission to elicit visceral and emotional responses in their readers through the fluidity of using sensory elements. The river serves as a conduit for rich imagery and complex descriptions, moving the reader's senses through the landscapes, characters, and events of the novel. Each sensory element, like tributaries merging into the main river, enriches the entire experience, producing a gripping and immersive narrative flow. The stream acts as a guide, directing writers in carefully blending sensory components to capture readers' emotions and bring the tale to life.

You see the transformational power of sensory nuances as you succumb to their stream. They become the threads that weave a sensory tapestry, allowing readers to see, hear, smell, taste, and touch the tale world. As readers are immersed into the narrative, experiencing its subtleties and immersing themselves in its sensory richness, the flow becomes a channel for emotional connection. Writers guarantee that their descriptions resound, elicit emotions, and leave a lasting impact by skillfully utilizing sensory details.

Sensory details shape the narrative's geography in the same way as the river carves its route through the terrain. They are responsible for the vivid colors, the harmonic symphony of noises, the enticing scents, the delicious tastes, and the palpable textures that bring the narrative to life. The flow of sensory elements acts as a driving force, influencing readers' perception and strengthening their connection with the story.

Writers tap into a fountain of creative potential by using sensory elements in a continuous, flowing rhythm. The river becomes a source of inspiration for authors, where they may immerse themselves in a variety of sensory sensations ranging from the whispering of leaves to the aroma of budding flowers, from the sizzling of a frying pan to the roughness of an aged wooden door. It enables the seamless integration of sensory descriptions, resulting in a story that immerses readers in a multi-sensory experience.

Using sensory details to improve descriptions is like immersing oneself in a never-ending river of bright sensations, where the currents of sight, sound, smell, taste, and touch blend flawlessly to create a rich and immersive storytelling experience. Sensory nuances build the fabric of a narrative, producing a multi-dimensional image that engages readers' senses and takes them into the world of the tale, much as the river meanders over varied landscapes.

Dive into the river of sensory details, allowing its currents to transport you on a trip of unforgettable sensations. This rushing stream depicts the palette of storytelling, where colors, sounds, scents, sensations, and textures merge together to bring the story to life. Each sensory detail blends into the next, resulting in a constant flow of feelings that capture readers' imaginations.

Writers engage on a mission to elicit visceral and emotional responses in their readers through the fluidity of using sensory elements. The river serves as a conduit for rich imagery and complex descriptions, moving the reader's senses through the landscapes, characters, and events of the novel. Each sensory element, like tributaries merging into the main river, enriches the entire experience, producing a gripping and immersive narrative flow. The stream acts as a guide, directing writers in carefully blending sensory components to capture readers' emotions and bring the tale to life.

Allow yourself to be carried away by the stream of sensory details and see their transformational power. They become the threads that weave a sensory tapestry, allowing readers to see, hear, smell, taste, and touch the tale world. As readers are immersed into the narrative, experiencing its subtleties and immersing themselves in its sensory richness, the flow becomes a channel for emotional connection. Writers guarantee that their descriptions resound, elicit emotions, and leave a lasting impact by skillfully utilizing sensory details.

Sensory details shape the narrative's geography in the same way as the river carves its route through the terrain. They are responsible for the vivid colors, the harmonic symphony of noises, the enticing scents, the delicious tastes, and the palpable textures that bring the narrative to life. The flow of sensory elements acts as a driving force, influencing readers' perception and strengthening their connection with the story.

Writers tap into a fountain of creative potential by using sensory elements in a continuous, flowing rhythm. The river becomes a source of inspiration for authors, where they may immerse themselves in a variety of sensory sensations ranging from the whispering of leaves to the aroma of budding flowers, from the sizzling of a frying pan to the roughness of an aged wooden door. It enables the seamless integration of sensory descriptions, resulting in a story that immerses readers in a multi-sensory experience.

Using sensory details to improve descriptions is like immersing oneself in a never-ending river of bright sensations, where the currents of sight, sound, smell, taste, and touch blend flawlessly to create a rich and immersive storytelling experience. Imagine jumping into the river and letting the stream transport you on a sensory voyage.

You become vividly aware of the importance of sensory elements in storytelling as you yield to the flowing river. The river serves as a conduit for rich visual and sensory sensations, leading readers through the story's landscapes, people, and events. The current binds together the sights, sounds, scents, tastes, and sensations that bring the story to life.

Writers begin on a mission to engage readers' senses and elicit emotional reactions through the fluidity of exploiting sensory information. The river serves as a source of inspiration, offering a plethora of descriptive choices. Each sensory element blends into the next, providing a continuous flow of experiences that transports readers into the story's core.

When you surrender to the river of sensory details, you may see their transformational power. They become the narrative's building elements, infusing it with realism and complexity. Sensory nuances affect the narrative's universe, giving levels of depth and immersing readers in a multi-dimensional experience, much as the river alters the surrounding environment.

The seamless incorporation into the story is ensured by the constant, flowing rhythm of adding sensory elements. The river acts as a guide, directing writers to carefully insert sensory components at the appropriate times. The current becomes a compass, assisting authors in creating vivid word pictures that appeal to readers' senses and capture their imaginations.

You observe how each sensory feature lends a distinct flavor to the tale as you navigate the river of sensory details. Colors dance before your eyes, sounds echo in your ears, smells waft through the air, tastes tempt your taste buds, and textures come to life beneath your touch. Readers are drawn further into the story's universe by the stream of sensory information.

Sensory nuances build the narrative's geography within the flowing river, creating a vivid backdrop for the characters and events to develop. The flow of sensory elements becomes the driving force, influencing readers' perceptions and emotions and helping them to connect with the tale on a deeper level.

Accept the art of using sensory details and let the flowing river to lead you on a transforming narrative adventure. Allow the current to lead you on a journey of vivid pictures, compelling descriptions, and emotional connections. Allow your tale to come alive with sights, sounds, scents, tastes, and textures by surrendering to the flow of introducing sensory aspects. Allow your readers to be captivated by the river of sensory information, immersing them in a world that engages all of their senses and creates a lasting impact.

Creating Believable and Evocative Environments

Creating convincing and evocative landscapes is like immersing oneself in a never-ending river of world-building, where the currents of authenticity and imagination blend perfectly, forming a dynamic and fascinating narrative experience. The development of places in stories, like the river, includes smoothly integrating genuine components with imagined details to take readers to vivid and captivating realms.

Consider delving into the river of believable and evocative settings, allowing its currents to carry you through a kaleidoscope of sights, sounds, scents, tastes, and sensations. This rushing stream exemplifies the skill of world-building, in which the synthesis of sensory data and mental conceptions serves as the foundation for a dramatic tale. Each element works in unison to provide a continuous flow of descriptions that engage readers' senses and transport them to the story's settings.

Writers start on a creative journey of developing worlds that seem real and compelling inside the flexibility of crafting habitats. The river serves as a conduit for genuine details, cultural subtleties, and intricately knit surroundings that anchor the story in realism.

Each piece of the landscape blends, providing a smooth and immersive narrative flow, much like tributaries merging into the main river. The stream becomes a compass, prompting authors to carefully balance familiarity and inventiveness in order to immerse readers in the world of the novel.

Allow yourself to be carried along by the tide of building believable and evocative places and observe their transformational power. They serve as the setting for the characters and events, defining the mood and impacting the reader's emotional connection to the tale. As readers explore elaborately depicted landscapes, immerse themselves in cultural subtleties, and imagine the story's environs, the flow becomes a channel for their imagination.

Environments influence the narrative's backdrop in the same way as the river carves its route through the terrain. They provide the elements that bring the tale world to life, from the busy streets of a bustling metropolis to the quiet tranquillity of a remote forest. The stream of plausible and evocative settings becomes the driving force, leading readers' absorption and enhancing their participation with the story.

Writers feed on a fountain of creativity and observation inside the continuous, fluid rhythm of producing surroundings. The river provides a source of inspiration for authors, allowing them to create realistic and vivid settings by drawing on real-world experiences, research, and imagination. It enables the smooth mixing of recognizable themes with inventive twists, resulting in a narrative that inspires readers to immerse themselves in the story's worlds and explore their depths.

Creating convincing and evocative landscapes is like immersing oneself in a never-ending river of world-building, where the currents of authenticity and imagination blend perfectly, forming a dynamic and fascinating narrative experience. Consider plunging into a river and letting the stream transport you through a tapestry of intense sensory sensations.

You become vividly aware of the influence of environment in narrative as you submit to the rushing river. The river becomes a medium for creating immersive environments, with the blending of genuine features and creative aspects serving as the narrative's backdrop. The current intertwines the sights, sounds, scents, tastes, and sensations that bring the environs to life.

Writers engage on a trip to capture the spirit of a location and transfer readers there inside the fluidity of constructing surroundings. The river is transformed into a conduit for ethnic richness, evocative descriptions, and imaginative scenery. Each piece blends into the next, resulting in a constant flow of details that engage readers' senses and immerse them in the world of the tale.

Surrendering to the current of building believable and evocative places allows you to observe the transformational power of these environments. They serve as a canvas for the people and events that occur, creating the scene and determining the tone of the story. Environments shape the narrative's world in the same way as the river shapes the surrounding terrain, offering a feeling of authenticity and immersing the reader in a concrete experience.

The constant, fluid rhythm of creating locations enables a seamless integration into the story. The river becomes a guiding force, urging writers to strike a delicate balance between descriptive richness and artistic flare. The current acts as a guide, allowing authors to construct vivid pictures with words, eliciting emotions and establishing a feeling of location that readers can relate to.

You note how each feature contributes to the overall ambiance as you traverse the river of believable and evocative locations. The scenery unfolds in front of your eyes, sounds resonate in your ears, fragrances fill the air, flavors dance on your tongue, and textures come to life beneath your hands. The current of surroundings envelops readers, pulling them further into the world of the novel.

Environments construct the narrative's backdrop inside the flowing river, offering a feeling of location and immersing the reader in a concrete experience. The current of believable and evocative landscapes becomes the driving force, influencing readers' senses and emotions and helping them to become totally immersed in the tale.

Creating convincing and evocative landscapes is like floating down a river of world-building, where the currents of authenticity and imagination blend perfectly, forming a dynamic and fascinating narrative experience. As you dive into this river, envision yourself being pulled along by its swift currents, bringing the settings of your novel to life.

Each feature within the flowing river helps to the creation of a genuine and immersive scene. As genuine features and imagined details merge together, the river becomes a medium for conveying the spirit of a location. It's a steady stream of descriptive richness that engages the reader's senses and draws them into the story's settings.

Surrendering to the current of building credible and evocative surroundings allows you to experience their transformational force. Each environment is transformed into a tapestry of sights, sounds, scents, tastes, and textures that engulf the reader's mind. The flow helps you through the process of effortlessly incorporating these elements, helping readers to immerse themselves in the story's universe, experiencing its distinct mood and beautiful sceneries.

Environments influence the backdrop of the story as the river carves its way across numerous geographies. They give the reader a sense of location, immersing them in a physical and unified experience. As readers get completely immersed in the story's surroundings, the current of believable and evocative locations becomes the driving force, influencing their perception and emotions.

Accept the challenge of creating genuine and evocative places, and let the river lead you on a transforming voyage of world-building. The current acts as a guide, prompting you to carefully balance detailed veracity with inventive flare. You have the ability to build amazing pictures with words, provoke emotions, and transport readers to new and exciting realms inside this river.

The landscapes come to life before your eyes as you negotiate the river's currents. You see the expansive vistas, hear the reverberating noises, smell the tantalizing fragrances, taste the unique tastes, and feel the textures beneath your hands. These sensory nuances are woven together by the current of settings, providing a unified and captivating narrative experience.

You get into a fountain of inspiration by working in this continuous, flowing rhythm of building convincing and compelling landscapes. The river becomes a source of inspiration, providing limitless opportunities to discover cultural subtleties, architectural marvels, natural vistas, and visionary universes. It enables seamless integration, allowing for the creation of worlds that connect with readers, take them further into the tale, and leave a lasting impact.

Accept the challenge of creating believable and evocative places, and let the rushing river transport you on a transforming voyage of world-building. Allow the current to lead you as you investigate sensory details, cultural nuances, and creative conceptions. Allow yourself to get carried away by the flow of creating surroundings that take readers, balancing authenticity and imagination to create fascinating universes. Allow your readers to be captivated by the flow of believable and vivid surroundings, bringing them to places they've never visited and leaving a lasting impression.

Using Settings to Convey Mood and Atmosphere

Setting mood and atmosphere is like navigating a continuous, flowing river of atmospheric materials, where the currents of descriptive details blend smoothly, forming a dynamic and emotive narrative experience. Setting in narrative, like the river, becomes the canvas on which emotions and ambience are painted, immersing readers in a vivid and engaging universe.

Imagine diving into a river of settings and letting the currents transport you on a sensory adventure. This flowing stream symbolizes the art of setting construction, in which descriptive aspects like as lighting, weather, architecture, and natural surrounds merge perfectly, setting the scene for the emotional tone of the tale. Each piece blends into the next, resulting in a constant flow of evocative elements that take readers to the heart of the story.

Within the fluidity of employing locations, authors go on a journey to portray mood and atmosphere, relying on descriptive language to elicit emotions and create the tone. The river serves as a conduit for powerful images, carrying readers through the landscapes, buildings, and natural surroundings of the novel.

Each piece of the scene converges into the primary stream, providing a seamless and immersive narrative flow. The stream acts as a compass, guiding authors in expertly producing details that elicit readers' emotions and enhance their connection to the tale.

Accept the current trend of employing settings to express mood and ambiance and experience their transformational impact. They serve as a background for the characters and events that unfold, establishing a feeling of location that defines the emotional landscape of the tale. Setting, like the river, shapes the atmosphere of the narrative by giving visual and sensory signals that evoke various emotions and engage readers on an emotional level.

The use of locations in a continuous, flowing rhythm provides a smooth integration into the story. The river takes on the role of a guide, prompting authors to carefully choose and build descriptive pieces that create the ideal mood and atmosphere. The current transforms into a brush, allowing writers to paint vivid pictures with words, evoking experiences and emotions that readers can relate to.

You observe how each element contributes to the overall mood as you travel the river of settings. The lighting generates the colours, the weather provides the atmosphere, the architecture reflects the character, and the natural surrounds bring the story to life. The enveloping river of evocative details draws readers further into the story's universe and immerses them in its emotional terrain.

Setting shapes the narrative's backdrop inside the moving river, offering a feeling of time, location, and emotional resonance. The current of mood and atmosphere becomes the driving force, influencing readers' perceptions and emotions and helping them to experience the tale on a more immersive and deeper level.

Using settings to portray mood and atmosphere is like to floating down a river of descriptive components, where the currents of emotions and sensory details mix effortlessly, forming a dynamic and powerful story experience. Imagine plunging into this river and letting the water carry you along, immersed in the power of surroundings to weave an intriguing tapestry.

You become intensely aware of how settings become the canvas onto which emotions and ambience are created as you submit to the rushing river. The river serves as a conduit for emotive images, bringing readers through the landscapes, architecture, and natural environs that define the atmosphere of the story. The current ties together the colors, sounds, aromas, textures, and visual aspects that bring the story's atmosphere to life.

Writers engage on a journey to transport readers to a certain emotional environment through the flexibility of utilising settings. As descriptive aspects blend seamlessly, the river becomes a channel for capturing the soul of a location. Each piece melts into the next, resulting in a constant flow of evocative elements that engage readers' senses, arouse their emotions, and immerse them in the world of the tale.

Allowing yourself to be influenced by the current trend of employing settings to portray mood and ambiance allows you to observe their transformational potential. They serve as the backdrop against which the characters and events occur, establishing the scene and determining the overall tone of the story. Just as the river influences the surrounding terrain, the story's surroundings form the emotional landscape, laying the groundwork for readers to connect with its core.

The continual, fluid rhythm of constructing locations guarantees that they blend seamlessly into the story. The river acts as a guide, encouraging writers to carefully choose and weave descriptive elements that evoke the appropriate mood and atmosphere. The current transforms into a brush, allowing writers to paint beautiful pictures with words, creating feelings and emotions that readers find intensely moving.

You observe how each element contributes to the overall mood as you travel the river of settings. The lighting produces a warm or cool glow, the weather whispers secrets, the building speaks of history and character, and the natural surrounds bring the story to life. The enveloping flood of evocative details draws readers further into the story's universe, generating emotional responses and immersing them in its sensory tapestry.

Setting shapes the narrative's backdrop inside the moving river, offering a feeling of location and emotional resonance. The current of mood and atmosphere becomes the driving force, influencing readers' perceptions and emotions and helping them to experience the tale on a more immersive and deeper level.

Using settings to portray mood and atmosphere is like to floating down a river of descriptive components, where the currents of emotions and sensory details mix effortlessly, forming a dynamic and powerful story experience. Imagine plunging into this river and letting the water carry you along, immersed in the power of surroundings to weave an intriguing tapestry.

You become intensely aware of how settings become the canvas onto which emotions and ambience are created as you submit to the rushing river. The river serves as a conduit for emotive images, bringing readers through the landscapes, architecture, and natural environs that define the atmosphere of the story. The current ties together the colors, sounds, aromas, textures, and visual aspects that bring the story's atmosphere to life.

Writers engage on a journey to transport readers to a certain emotional environment through the flexibility of utilising settings. As descriptive aspects blend seamlessly, the river becomes a channel for capturing the soul of a location. Each piece melts into the next, resulting in a constant flow of evocative elements that engage readers' senses, arouse their emotions, and immerse them in the world of the tale.

Allowing yourself to be influenced by the current trend of employing settings to portray mood and ambiance allows you to observe their transformational potential. They serve as the backdrop against which the characters and events occur, establishing the scene and determining the overall tone of the story. Just as the river influences the surrounding terrain, the story's surroundings form the emotional landscape, laying the groundwork for readers to connect with its core.

The continual, fluid rhythm of constructing locations guarantees that they blend seamlessly into the story. The river acts as a guide, encouraging writers to carefully choose and weave descriptive elements that evoke the appropriate mood and atmosphere. The current transforms into a brush, allowing writers to paint beautiful pictures with words, creating feelings and emotions that readers find intensely moving.

You observe how each element contributes to the overall mood as you travel the river of settings. The lighting produces a warm or cool glow, the weather whispers secrets, the building speaks of history and character, and the natural surrounds bring the story to life. The enveloping flood of evocative details draws readers further into the story's universe, generating emotional responses and immersing them in its sensory tapestry.

Setting shapes the narrative's backdrop inside the moving river, offering a feeling of location and emotional resonance. The current of mood and atmosphere becomes the driving force, influencing readers' perceptions and emotions and helping them to experience the tale on a more immersive and deeper level.

Accept the art of employing surroundings to express mood and ambiance, and let the flowing river to transport you on a transforming storytelling trip. Allow the stream to lead you through your examination of descriptive details, sensory signals, and emotional complexity. Allow yourself to get carried away by the fluidity of creating settings that transport readers while blending rich imagery with emotional relevance. Allow your readers to be captivated by the river of atmospheric details, producing an immersive and evocative experience that stays long after they've turned the final page.

Chapter 6: Mastering Point of View
Exploring Different Narrative Perspectives

Exploring many narrative viewpoints is like swimming down a never-ending river of storytelling possibilities, where the currents of point of view combine fluidly, forming a dynamic and diverse narrative experience. Narrative perspectives, like the river, give distinct vantage points from which the tale unfolds, resulting in a rich and diverse storytelling tapestry.

Consider delving into the river of narrative perspectives and allowing its currents to take you on a trip of many points of view. This flowing stream symbolizes the art of storytelling, in which narrative voices and views combine seamlessly, creating the reader's interpretation of the story. Each viewpoint blends into the next, resulting in a constant flow of storytelling options that captivate readers' brains and immerse them in the narrative universe.

Writers go on a creative examination of character voices, personal experiences, and varied viewpoints within the flexibility of exploring narrative perspectives. The river serves as a conduit for storytelling possibilities, taking readers through the story's many lenses. Each perspective, like tributaries merging into the main channel, adds depth and complexity, resulting in a seamless and immersive narrative flow. The stream acts as a compass, guiding writers in selecting the most effective perspective to express their tale.

Allow yourself to be carried along by the tide of studying multiple story viewpoints and observe their transformational impact. They serve as a window into the tale, providing unique insights and emotional connections. Just as the river carves its way through the terrain, narrative perspectives create the core of the story, creating a complex tapestry of voices and points of view that engage readers.

The fluid rhythm of investigating narrative viewpoints enables a smooth incorporation into the story. The river takes on the role of a guide, taking authors through the complicated interplay of voices and opinions. The current transforms into a brush, allowing writers to paint vivid people and events, eliciting empathy and immersing readers in the story's richness and complexity.

You observe how each decision changes the reader's experience as you travel the river of narrative viewpoints. The point of view becomes a prism through which the story world is exposed, creating the emotional connection and comprehension of the story. The current of narrative viewpoints envelops readers, dragging them further into the world of the tale, creating empathy, and inviting them to perceive the story from several perspectives.

Narrative perspectives construct the narrative's backdrop inside the flowing river, giving a mosaic of voices and experiences. The current of multiple points of view becomes the driving force, influencing readers' perceptions and emotions and helping them to connect with the tale from various perspectives and comprehend its complexity.

Exploring many narrative viewpoints is like swimming down a never-ending river of storytelling possibilities, where the currents of point of view combine fluidly, forming a dynamic and diverse narrative experience. The river takes you on a voyage via several perspectives, each lending its own distinct flavor to the tale tapestry.

You get involved in the art of storytelling as you yield to the flowing river, where the fusion of narrative voices and views produces a rich and engaging narrative experience. The river links together the numerous views, fluidly shifting from one to the next, providing readers with a never-ending stream of storytelling options that engage their thoughts and excite their imagination.

Within the flexibility of investigating narrative viewpoints, authors delve into the minds, feelings, and experiences of several individuals. The river serves as a conduit for these many points of view, taking readers across a wide spectrum of perspectives. Each point of view combines with the next, resulting in a never-ending stream of storytelling possibilities that fascinate readers and draw them into the world of the story.

Surrendering to the stream of investigating many story viewpoints helps you to observe the transformational power of these choices. Each point of view becomes a window into the tale, providing new insights and eliciting emotional responses. Just as the river carves its way through the landscape, narrative perspectives form the core of the tale, creating a tapestry of voices and perspectives that capture readers and bring the story to life.

The fluid rhythm of investigating narrative viewpoints enables a smooth incorporation into the story. The river becomes a guiding force, directing authors to traverse the complicated interplay of views with finesse. The current transforms into a brush, allowing writers to paint vivid people and events, eliciting empathy and immersing readers in the story's richness and complexity.

You observe how each decision changes the reader's experience as you travel the river of narrative viewpoints. The point of view becomes a prism through which the story world is exposed, creating the emotional connection and comprehension of the story. The current of narrative viewpoints envelops readers, dragging them further into the world of the tale, developing empathy, and providing new insights from multiple views.

Narrative perspectives construct the narrative's backdrop inside the flowing river, giving a mosaic of voices and experiences. The current of several points of view becomes the driving force, leading readers' perceptions and emotions, allowing them to connect with the tale from numerous perspectives and comprehend its complexity.

Exploring many narrative viewpoints is like swimming down a never-ending river of storytelling possibilities, where the currents of point of view combine fluidly, forming a dynamic and diverse narrative experience. Consider jumping into this river and allowing its currents to transport you through a trip of diverse perspectives, each adding depth and texture to the storytelling tapestry.

You become intensely aware of how narrative viewpoints impact the way a tale is delivered as you submit to the flowing river. The river serves as a conduit for many voices, opinions, and experiences, taking readers through a kaleidoscope of perspectives. The current smoothly links different views together, resulting in a never-ending stream of storytelling options that captivate readers' brains and welcome them into the narrative universe.

Writers take on a creative examination of character psychology, personal histories, and distinct glasses through which to see the story within the flexibility of exploring narrative viewpoints. The river becomes a conduit for narrative possibilities, with each point of view contributing to the larger narrative fabric. Each point of view melts into the main river like tributaries, resulting in a smooth and immersive narrative flow. The stream acts as a compass, assisting authors in selecting the most effective perspective to tell their tale.

Allow yourself to be carried along by the tide of studying multiple story viewpoints and observe their transformational impact. They become the filters through which the tale is filtered, each with their own set of insights, prejudices, and emotions. The river carves its route through the environment, and narrative viewpoints create the substance of the tale, giving a diverse and interesting reading experience.

The seamless incorporation into the story is ensured by the continual, flowing rhythm of building narrative viewpoints. The river serves as a guide, taking authors through the difficulties of each viewpoint. The current acts as a brush, allowing authors to paint vivid people and situations, eliciting empathy and immersing readers in the story's distinct views.

You observe how each decision changes the reader's experience as you travel the river of narrative viewpoints. The point of view acts as a doorway, taking readers inside the thoughts and emotions of the characters, providing insights and throwing light on various facets of the tale. The current of narrative viewpoints envelops readers, dragging them deeper into the world of the story and encouraging connection and empathy.

Within the flowing river, narrative views create the backdrop of the story, creating a complex tapestry of voices and experiences. The current of many viewpoints becomes the driving force, leading readers' perceptions and emotions and helping them to connect with the tale from several perspectives and obtain a thorough grasp of its complexities.

Allow the flowing river to lead you on a transforming storytelling trip as you embrace the art of exploring diverse narrative viewpoints. Allow the current to lead your investigation of character voices, distinct perspectives, and storytelling options. Allow yourself to get carried away by the fluidity of creating narratives that transport readers, blending many views to create a rich and nuanced narrative tapestry. Allow your readers to be captivated by the river of narrative viewpoints, providing them with a rich and deep experience that will stay with them long after they've done reading.

Choosing the Right Point of View for Your Story

Choosing the best point of view for your tale is like to navigating a continuous, flowing river of narrative viewpoint, where the currents of storytelling alternatives mix fluidly, forming a dynamic and fascinating narrative experience. The point of view, like the river, becomes the prism through which the tale unfolds, providing readers with a distinct vantage point and influencing their interpretation of the narrative.

Consider delving into the river of point of view and allowing its currents to lead you on a voyage of narrative possibilities. This flowing stream symbolizes the art of storytelling, in which views and narrative voices combine smoothly, forming the reader's relationship to the story. Each viewpoint blends into the next, resulting in a constant flow of storytelling options that captivate readers' brains and immerse them in the narrative universe.

Writers embark on a creative examination of narrative voice, character closeness, and reader involvement within the fluidity of picking the proper point of view. The river serves as a conduit for tale ideas, directing authors through the many alternatives. Each perspective, like tributaries merging into the main channel, adds depth and intimacy to the tale, resulting in a smooth and immersive flow. The stream acts as a compass, guiding authors in picking the most effective point of view to portray their tale.

Surrender to the tide of selecting the correct point of view and see its transformational power. It becomes the portal through which readers experience the story, providing a distinct perspective on the events and characters. The selected point of view forms the narrative's core, giving the reader with a distinct viewpoint and emotional connection to the story, much as the river carves its route across the landscape.

The fluid rhythm of selecting the appropriate point of view enables a seamless integration into the story. The river serves as a guide, assisting authors in navigating the complexity of character viewpoints and reader involvement. The current transforms into a brush, allowing authors to paint beautiful verbal pictures, generating emotions and immersing readers in the selected point of view.

You observe how each option changes the reader's experience as you navigate the river of point of view. The reader's comprehension and emotional connection to the tale are shaped by the reader's knowledge and emotional connection to the characters' ideas, feelings, and motives. The current of point of view envelops readers, dragging them further into the story's universe, building empathy, and letting them to experience the tale intimately via the selected lens.

The appropriate point of view defines the narrative's backdrop inside the moving river, offering a lens through which the story unfolds. The current of perspective becomes the driving force, influencing readers' perceptions and emotions and helping them to interact with the tale on a more profound and engaging level.

Choosing the proper point of view for your tale is like floating down a river of narrative possibilities, where the currents of storytelling mix effortlessly, creating a dynamic and compelling narrative experience. Imagine plunging into this river and letting the currents take you on a voyage of perspective and immersion as the tale unfolds in front of you.

You become conscious of the power of point of view in narrative as you succumb to the flowing river. The river serves as a conduit for several lenses through which the tale can be delivered, each of which offers a distinct viewpoint and narrative experience. The current fluidly changes between multiple points of view, resulting in a never-ending stream of storytelling options that captivate readers' brains and immerse them in the narrative universe.

Writers go on a creative study of narrative voice, character depth, and reader connection within the fluidity of selecting the proper point of view. The river serves as a canvas for tale ideas, directing authors through the numerous alternatives. Each point of view, like tributaries merging into the main channel, adds richness and variety to the overall narrative. The stream acts as a compass, encouraging writers to choose the most effective perspective to tell their tale.

Surrender to the tide of selecting the correct point of view and see its transformational power. It transforms into the lens through which readers perceive the tale, affecting their comprehension and emotional connection. The selected point of view creates the substance of the tale, offering a distinct perspective and intimacy that connects with readers, just as the river carves its route across the environment.

The fluid rhythm of selecting the appropriate point of view enables a seamless integration into the story. The river serves as a guide, helping writers through the complexity of character viewpoints and reader involvement. The current is transformed into a brush, allowing authors to paint amazing pictures with words, generating emotions and immersing readers in the selected viewpoint.

You observe how each option changes the reader's experience as you navigate the river of point of view. The viewpoint transforms into a window into the characters' thoughts, motives, and experiences, influencing the reader's comprehension and emotional connection to the tale. The current of point of view envelops readers, dragging them further into the world of the tale, encouraging empathy, and letting them to perceive the narrative through the selected lens.

The appropriate point of view sets the narrative's backdrop inside the moving river, presenting the reader with a distinct vantage point. The current of perspective becomes the driving force, influencing readers' perceptions and emotions and helping them to interact with the tale on a more profound and engaging level.

Choosing the proper point of view for your tale is like floating down a river of narrative possibilities, where the currents of storytelling mix effortlessly, creating a dynamic and compelling narrative experience. Imagine plunging into this river and letting the currents take you on a voyage of perspective and immersion as the tale unfolds in front of you.

You become conscious of the power of point of view in narrative as you succumb to the flowing river. The river serves as a conduit for several lenses through which the tale can be delivered, each of which offers a distinct viewpoint and narrative experience. The current fluidly changes between multiple points of view, resulting in a never-ending stream of storytelling options that captivate readers' brains and immerse them in the narrative universe.

Writers go on a creative study of narrative voice, character depth, and reader connection within the fluidity of selecting the proper point of view. The river serves as a canvas for tale ideas, directing authors through the numerous alternatives. Each point of view, like tributaries merging into the main channel, adds richness and variety to the overall narrative. The stream acts as a compass, encouraging writers to choose the most effective perspective to tell their tale.

Surrender to the tide of selecting the correct point of view and see its transformational power. It transforms into the lens through which readers perceive the tale, affecting their comprehension and emotional connection. The selected point of view creates the substance of the tale, offering a distinct perspective and intimacy that connects with readers, just as the river carves its route across the environment.

The fluid rhythm of selecting the appropriate point of view enables a seamless integration into the story. The river serves as a guide, helping writers through the complexity of character viewpoints and reader involvement. The current is transformed into a brush, allowing authors to paint amazing pictures with words, generating emotions and immersing readers in the selected viewpoint.

You observe how each option changes the reader's experience as you navigate the river of point of view. The viewpoint transforms into a window into the characters' thoughts, motives, and experiences, influencing the reader's comprehension and emotional connection to the tale. The current of point of view envelops readers, dragging them further into the world of the tale, encouraging empathy, and letting them to perceive the narrative through the selected lens.

The appropriate point of view sets the narrative's backdrop inside the moving river, presenting the reader with a distinct vantage point. The current of perspective becomes the driving force, influencing readers' perceptions and emotions and helping them to interact with the tale on a more profound and engaging level.

Accept the art of selecting the appropriate point of view and let the flowing river to transport you on a transforming narrative adventure. Allow the stream to lead you as you investigate narrative voice, character viewpoints, and reader connection. Allow yourself to get carried away by the fluidity of producing narratives that transport readers, mixing intimacy and involvement to produce a fascinating and true storytelling experience. Allow your readers to be captivated by the river of point of view, providing them with a unique and engaging perspective that will echo long after they've turned the final page.

Harnessing Point of View for Characterization and Immersion

Using point of view for characterisation and immersion is akin to floating down a river of narrative viewpoint, where the currents of storytelling mix fluidly, creating a dynamic and engaging reading experience. Consider plunging into this river and letting the currents sweep you along, immersing yourself in the power of point of view to create vivid characters and a compelling narrative universe.

As you submit to the current, you become intensely aware of how point of view becomes the prism through which readers perceive and relate with the characters in the tale. The river serves as a conduit for readers to explore their ideas, feelings, and experiences, allowing them to get intimately acquainted with their inner world. The current smoothly knits together the character's point of view and the reader's comprehension, resulting in a constant flow of characterisation and immersion.

Writers start on a creative investigation of character depth and reader involvement within the flexibility of harnessing point of view. The river serves as a conduit for storytelling options, aiding authors in selecting the most effective point of view to show the complexities of their characters. Each perspective, like tributaries merging into the main channel, adds a layer of depth to the characters, resulting in a smooth and engaging narrative flow. The stream becomes a compass, guiding authors to navigate the currents of point of view in order to create realistic and captivating character depictions.

Surrender to the tide of harnessing point of view and experience its transformational power in characterisation and immersion. It becomes a window through which readers may see the characters' world, their thoughts, motives, and evolution. The selected point of view molds the narrative's core, offering a distinct and intimate connection to the characters, just as the river carves its route through the terrain.

The perfect incorporation into the story is ensured by the continual, flowing rhythm of each point of view. The river acts as a guide, encouraging writers to go deeply into the character's point of view, capturing their voice, and immersing readers in their emotional journey. The current is transformed into a brush, allowing writers to create rich and detailed character portraits, eliciting empathy and building a deep link between readers and the characters of the tale.

You observe how each option changes the reader's experience as you navigate the river of point of view. The point of view serves as a channel for comprehending the character's aspirations, anxieties, and conflicts, establishing a direct relationship to their emotional environment. The current of point of view envelops readers, dragging them further into the world of the character, cultivating empathy, and allowing them to walk in their shoes.

Harnessing point of view builds the narrative's setting inside the moving river, creating a lens through which the characters come to life. The current of perspective becomes the driving force, leading readers' perceptions and emotions and helping them to fully immerse themselves in the adventure of the character.

Using point of view for characterisation and immersion is akin to floating down a river of narrative viewpoint, where the currents of storytelling mix fluidly, creating a dynamic and engaging reading experience. Consider plunging into this river and letting the currents sweep you along, immersing yourself in the power of point of view to create vivid characters and a compelling narrative universe.

As you submit to the current, you become intensely aware of how point of view becomes the prism through which readers perceive and relate with the characters in the tale. The river serves as a conduit for readers to explore their ideas, feelings, and experiences, allowing them to get intimately acquainted with their inner world. The current smoothly knits together the character's point of view and the reader's comprehension, resulting in a constant flow of characterisation and immersion.

Writers start on a creative investigation of character depth and reader involvement within the flexibility of harnessing point of view. The river serves as a conduit for storytelling options, aiding authors in selecting the most effective point of view to show the complexities of their characters. Each perspective, like tributaries merging into the main channel, adds a layer of depth to the characters, resulting in a smooth and engaging narrative flow. The stream becomes a compass, guiding authors to navigate the currents of point of view in order to create realistic and captivating character depictions.

Surrender to the tide of harnessing point of view and experience its transformational power in characterisation and immersion. It becomes a window through which readers may see the characters' world, their thoughts, motives, and evolution. The selected point of view molds the narrative's core, offering a distinct and intimate connection to the characters, just as the river carves its route through the terrain.

The perfect incorporation into the story is ensured by the continual, flowing rhythm of each point of view. The river acts as a guide, encouraging writers to go deeply into the character's point of view, capturing their voice, and immersing readers in their emotional journey. The current is transformed into a brush, allowing writers to create rich and detailed character portraits, eliciting empathy and building a deep link between readers and the characters of the tale.

You observe how each option changes the reader's experience as you navigate the river of point of view. The point of view serves as a channel for comprehending the character's aspirations, anxieties, and conflicts, establishing a direct relationship to their emotional environment. The current of point of view envelops readers, dragging them further into the world of the character, cultivating empathy, and allowing them to walk in their shoes.

Harnessing point of view builds the narrative's setting inside the moving river, creating a lens through which the characters come to life. The current of perspective becomes the driving force, leading readers' perceptions and emotions and helping them to fully immerse themselves in the adventure of the character.

Harnessing point of view for characterisation and immersion in storytelling is analogous to navigating a continuous, flowing river of narrative viewpoint. This river symbolizes the ever-present stream that sweeps readers along, immersing them in the story's universe and letting them to interact with the characters on an intimate level.

You become aware of how point of view becomes the prism through which readers see the tale as you submit to the flowing river. It is an effective tool for shaping their comprehension and emotional connection to the characters. The currents of the river combine smoothly with the story, producing a continuous flow of characterisation and immersion.

Writers start on a creative investigation of character depth and reader involvement within the flexibility of harnessing point of view. The river serves as a conduit for several viewpoints, aiding authors in selecting the most effective vantage point to bring their characters to life. Each point of view, like tributaries merging into the main channel, adds a layer of richness to the overall narrative flow. The stream becomes a compass, guiding authors to navigate the currents of point of view in order to create realistic and captivating character depictions.

Surrendering to the tide of harnessing point of view enables you to experience its transformational power in characterisation and immersion. It acts as a conduit, allowing readers access to the characters' inner thoughts, feelings, and experiences. The selected point of view forms the narrative's core, creating a distinct and intimate link to the characters' lives, just as the river carves its route through the terrain.

The perfect incorporation into the story is ensured by the continual, flowing rhythm of each point of view. The river becomes a driving force, urging writers to go deeply into the character's point of view, capturing their voice and immersing readers in their world. The current is transformed into a brush, allowing writers to create vivid and detailed character portraits, eliciting empathy and building a deep link between readers and the characters of the tale.

You observe how each option changes the reader's experience as you navigate the river of point of view. The point of view serves as a channel for understanding the characters' motives, anxieties, and desires, providing a direct link to their emotional journey. The stream of point of view engulfs readers, dragging them further into the world of the character, developing empathy and allowing them to share in their pleasures, losses, and victories.

Harnessing point of view builds the narrative's setting inside the moving river, creating a lens through which the characters come to life. The current of perspective becomes the driving force, leading readers' perceptions and emotions and helping them to become totally immersed in the character's experience.

Accept the art of using point of view to create characterisation and immersion, and let the river transport you on a profound narrative adventure. Allow yourself to get carried away by the fluidity of creating narratives that transport readers, blending intimacy and involvement to build real and relatable characters. Allow your readers to be captivated by the river of point of view, providing them with an immersive experience that enhances their connection to the tale and its heroes.

Chapter 7: The Power of Language
Developing a Distinctive Writing Style

Creating a distinct writing style is similar to floating through a continuous river of creative expression, where the currents of language and imagination blend smoothly, forming a distinct and appealing literary voice. Consider plunging into this river and allowing the currents to take you along while you explore the depths of your creativity and enhance your artistic expression.

You become intensely aware of the power of language and the creativity of words as you succumb to the flowing river. The river acts as a channel for your feelings, emotions, and ideas, allowing your uniqueness to show through. The current smoothly knits your literary choices together, resulting in a continuous flow of writing that is uniquely yours.

You go on a creative journey of self-discovery and experimentation as you build a distinct writing style. The river serves as a blank canvas for your creative creations, guiding you through different writing approaches, shapes, and structures. Each piece, like tributaries merging into the main channel, provides a layer of originality, contributing to the overall flow of your work. The stream acts as a compass, guiding you through the currents of creation and refining your style.

Allow yourself to be carried along by the tide of establishing a distinct writing style and observe its transformational force. It becomes the prism through which readers interpret your work, distinguishing you from the competition in the literary environment. Your writing style forms the core of your words, delivering a personal and recognized touch that connects with readers, just as the river carves its route through the environment.

The continual, flowing rhythm of building a distinct writing style guarantees that your voice is seamlessly integrated into the story. The river acts as a guide, supporting you in fine-tuning your language choices, sentence patterns, and storytelling strategies. The current transforms into a brush, allowing you to paint stunning images and elicit emotions with your unique creative ability.

You see how each option effects your readers' experience as you navigate the river of building a distinct writing style. Your writing style becomes a doorway into your literary universe, communicating your own viewpoints, topics, and feelings. Your writing style engulfs readers, dragging them further into your story, engaging their imaginations, and immersing them in the core of your creative vision.

Developing a particular writing style inside the flowing river defines the backdrop of your literary universe, offering a lens through which your stories emerge. Your style's current becomes the driving force, influencing readers' perceptions and emotions and helping them to fully understand your distinct voice and aesthetic expression.

Creating a distinct writing style is like swimming through a never-ending river of creative expression, where the currents of language and imagination mix smoothly, forming a distinct and engaging literary voice. Imagine plunging into this river and allowing its currents to take you as you explore the depths of your imagination and enhance your artistic expression.

You become intensely aware of the power of language and the creativity of words as you succumb to the flowing river. The river acts as a channel for your thoughts, feelings, and ideas, letting your unique personality to show through in each sentence and paragraph. The current seamlessly knits your literary choices together, resulting in a continuous flow of literature that carries your individual mark.

You go on a voyage of self-discovery and creative exploration as you build a distinct writing style. The river serves as a canvas for your text, guiding you through various writing approaches, literary devices, and story structures. Each piece, like tributaries merging into the main channel, provides a layer of originality, contributing to the overall flow of your work. The stream transforms into a compass, leading you through the currents of inspiration and refining your style with aim and purpose.

Allow yourself to be carried along by the tide of establishing a distinct writing style and observe its transformational force. It becomes the prism through which your work is perceived by readers, allowing them to recognize your voice in a sea of words. Your writing style, like the river, carves its own route across the literary landscape, leaving a particular trace that distinguishes you.

The continual, flowing rhythm of building a distinct writing style guarantees that your voice is seamlessly integrated into the story.

The river acts as a guide, influencing your language choices, sentence patterns, and storytelling tactics. With your particular artistic flare, the current transforms into a brush, allowing you to paint amazing images, generate emotions, and transmit thoughts.

You see how each option effects the reader's experience as you navigate the river of building a distinct writing style. Your writing style becomes a doorway into your literary universe, displaying your own ideas, topics, and insights. Your writing style envelops readers, dragging them further into the story, capturing their imaginations, and immersing them in the core of your creative vision.

Developing a particular writing style within the flowing river defines the backdrop of your literary world, offering a lens through which your stories emerge. Your style's current becomes the driving force, molding readers' thoughts and emotions and helping them to fully comprehend and connect with your distinctive voice and artistic expression.

Creating a distinct writing style is similar to navigating a continuous, flowing river of creative expression, where the currents of language and imagination blend effortlessly, forming a distinct and appealing literary voice. Consider immersing yourself in this river, allowing its currents to transport you while you explore the depths of your creativity and enhance your artistic expression.

You become intensely aware of the power of language and the creativity of words as you succumb to the flowing river. The river acts as a channel for your thoughts, feelings, and ideas, letting your uniqueness to shine through each line and paragraph. The current seamlessly knits your literary choices together, resulting in a continuous flow of text that reflects your individual identity.

You go on a voyage of self-discovery and creative exploration as you build a distinct writing style. The river serves as a canvas for your text, guiding you through various writing approaches, literary devices, and story structures. Each piece, like tributaries merging into the main channel, provides a layer of originality, contributing to the overall flow of your work. The stream acts as a compass, guiding you through the currents of inspiration and refining your style with aim and purpose.

Allow yourself to be carried along by the tide of establishing a distinct writing style and observe its transformational force. It becomes the prism through which your work is perceived by readers, allowing them to recognize your voice in a sea of words. Your writing style, like the river, carves its own route across the literary landscape, leaving a particular trace that distinguishes you.

The continual, flowing rhythm of building a distinct writing style guarantees that your voice is seamlessly integrated into the story. The river acts as a guide, influencing your language choices, sentence patterns, and storytelling tactics. With your particular artistic flare, the current transforms into a brush, allowing you to paint amazing images, generate emotions, and transmit thoughts.

You see how each option effects the reader's experience as you navigate the river of building a distinct writing style. Your writing style becomes a doorway into your literary universe, displaying your own ideas, topics, and insights. Your writing style envelops readers, dragging them further into the story, capturing their imaginations, and immersing them in the core of your creative vision.

Developing a particular writing style within the flowing river defines the backdrop of your literary world, offering a lens through which your stories emerge. Your style's current becomes the driving force, molding readers' thoughts and emotions and helping them to fully comprehend and connect with your distinctive voice and artistic expression.

Accept the challenge of building a distinct writing style and let the flowing river to transport you on a transforming creative trip. Allow your thoughts to flow, blending your originality with literary approaches to create a tapestry that is uniquely yours. Allow the river of your writing style to enthrall your readers, providing them with an immersive experience that connects with the strength and beauty of your own literary genius.

Using Figurative Language and Literary Devices

Using figurative language and literary techniques is like floating down a river of expressive possibilities, where the currents of words and imagination blend smoothly to create a dynamic and compelling literary experience. Imagine plunging into this river and letting the currents take you along as you explore the depths of language and discover the power of narrative.

You become intensely aware of the power of metaphorical language and literary methods as you yield to the rushing river. The river transforms into a creative playground, allowing you to explore metaphors, similes, personification, and other literary devices. The current seamlessly ties these pieces together, providing a continuous flow of vibrant images and compelling sentiments that bring your work to life.

You begin on a voyage of creative inquiry and poetic resonance via the flexibility of employing figurative language and literary conventions. The river becomes a canvas for you to paint on, leading you through various approaches and structures. Each device, like tributaries flowing into the main channel, provides a layer of depth, contributing to the overall richness and impact of your work. The stream becomes a compass, guiding you through the currents of creation and pointing you to the most effective instruments for enhancing your narrative.

Allow yourself to be carried away by the tide of employing figurative language and literary devices, and observe their transformational power. They serve as the palette through which readers view your work, filling it with vibrant colors and inventive brushstrokes. Just as the river carves its own route through the environment, these devices carve their own distinctive path through the literary landscape, leaving an unforgettable imprint on the minds of readers.

The constant, flowing rhythm of employing figurative language and literary methods guarantees that poetic components are seamlessly integrated into the narrative. The river acts as a guide, influencing your language choices, sentence patterns, and storytelling tactics. With a skillful touch, the current transforms into a brush, allowing you to create beautiful scenes, elicit emotions, and captivate readers' senses.

You observe how each option effects the reader's experience as you navigate the river of employing figurative language and literary techniques. These gadgets serve as a doorway into a world of enhanced images and greater comprehension, catching readers' attention and immersing them in your story. The stream of figurative language envelops readers, pushing them closer to the core of your tale, kindling their imagination, and forging a deep connection.

Using figurative language and literary devices inside the flowing river builds the backdrop of your literary world, offering a lens through which your stories develop. The current of poetic expression becomes the driving force, guiding readers' perceptions and emotions so that they may completely appreciate the beauty and power of your words.

Using figurative language and literary techniques is like being swept along by a never-ending river of expressive possibilities, where the currents of words and imagination blend effortlessly to create a vivid and compelling literary experience. Imagine yourself diving into this river, its currents gently leading you along as you go on a journey to discover the depths of language and the full power of narrative.

You become intensely aware of the power of metaphorical language and literary methods as you yield to the rushing river. They become your buddies, your instruments for infusing richness, depth, and vividness into your work. The river transforms into a creative playground, where you may immerse yourself in metaphors, similes, personification, alliteration, and other literary jewels. The current seamlessly links these pieces together, providing a continuous flow of imagery, emotion, and impact that brings your text to life.

You begin on a voyage of inquiry and poetic resonance via the flexibility of employing figurative language and literary tropes. The river becomes your canvas, a huge expanse across which you paint with words in accordance with the rhythm and flow of your ideas. Each device, like tributaries merging into the main channel, adds a layer of depth and subtlety to the overall richness and beauty of your work. The stream becomes a compass, guiding you in the direction of inspiration, urging you to navigate the currents and select the most effective instruments to enrich your tale.

Allow yourself to be carried away by the tide of employing figurative language and literary devices, and observe their transformational power. They become the colors on your palette, the brushes in your fingers, as you paint beautiful scenarios and elicit emotional responses from your readers. These devices, like the river, cut their own route across the literary landscape, leaving an unforgettable impact on the minds and hearts of readers who dive into your work.

The constant, flowing rhythm of employing figurative language and literary devices guarantees that poetic aspects are seamlessly integrated into your story. The river guides you, influencing your language choices, phrase patterns, and story flow. The current transforms into a brush, allowing you to paint precisely, use imagery, symbolism, and other tactics to bring your words to life in the minds of your readers.

You observe how each option effects the reader's experience as you navigate the river of employing figurative language and literary techniques. These gadgets act as gateways, taking readers to a world of enhanced sensations, piqueing their imaginations, and prompting a better grasp of your content. The current of figurative language envelops readers, pushing them closer to the center of your tale and letting them to connect with the feelings and ideas you want to portray.

Using figurative language and literary devices inside the flowing river builds the backdrop of your literary universe, offering a lens through which your narrativetories unfold. The current of poetic expression becomes the driving force, shaping readers' perceptions and emotions, allowing them to fully appreciate the beauty and power of your words.

Using figurative language and literary devices is like being carried by a continuous, flowing river of expressive possibilities, where the currents of words and imagination merge seamlessly, shaping a vibrant and captivating literary experience. Imagine yourself diving into this river, feeling its currents gently guiding you along as you embark on a journey to explore the depths of language and unlock the true potential of storytelling.

As you surrender to the flowing river, you become acutely aware of the power of figurative language and literary devices. They become your allies, your artistic tools that breathe life into your writing. The river becomes a playground of creativity, where you can immerse yourself in metaphors, similes, personification, and other literary gems. The current effortlessly weaves together these elements, creating a continuous flow of imagery, emotion, and impact that enchants your readers.

Within the fluidity of using figurative language and literary devices, you embark on a poetic odyssey. The river becomes your canvas, an expansive space upon which you paint with words, guided by the rhythm and melody of your thoughts. Like tributaries converging into the main current, each device adds a layer of depth and nuance, contributing to the overall richness and beauty of your writing. The stream becomes your compass, encouraging you to navigate the currents, making intentional choices that enhance your storytelling.

Surrender to the current of using figurative language and literary devices, and witness their transformative power. They become the colors on your palette, the brushes in your hand, as you craft vivid scenes and evoke emotions in your readers. Just as the river carves its path through the landscape, these devices carve their own path through the literary landscape, leaving an indelible mark on the hearts and minds of those who immerse themselves in your work.

The continuous, flowing rhythm of using figurative language and literary devices ensures a seamless integration of poetic elements into your narrative. The river becomes your guide, shaping your language choices, sentence structures, and narrative flow. The current becomes a brush, allowing you to paint with precision, using imagery, symbolism, and other devices to illuminate your ideas and captivate your audience.

As you navigate the river of using figurative language and literary devices, you notice how each choice influences the reader's experience. These devices become portals, transporting readers to new realms of imagination and emotion, enriching their understanding and connection to your writing. The current of figurative language envelops readers, drawing them closer to the essence of your story, allowing them to experience its depth and resonance.

Within the flowing river, using figurative language and literary devices shapes the backdrop of your literary world, providing a lens through which your stories come alive. The current of poetic expression becomes the driving force, shaping readers' perceptions and emotions, allowing them to fully appreciate the beauty and power of your words.

Embrace the art of using figurative language and literary devices, and let the flowing river carry you on a transformative creative journey. Surrender to the fluidity of your words, allowing them to flow effortlessly and weave themselves into a tapestry of imagery and emotion. Let the river of your writing captivate your readers, inviting them to immerse themselves in a mesmerizing experience that resonates with the power, beauty, and depth of figurative language and literary devices.

Polishing Prose through Editing and Revision

Editing and revising text is like navigating a constant, flowing river of refinement, where the currents of examination and creativity blend effortlessly, becoming a polished and compelling written product. Consider jumping into this river, allowing its currents to gently lead you as you go on a journey to improve your work and raise it to its utmost potential.

You become vividly aware of the power of editing and rewriting as you submit to the flowing river. They become loyal partners, assisting you in removing the excess and revealing the actual substance of your work. The river transforms into a transformational area where you may practice the skill of word choice, phrase construction, clarity, and coherence. The current seamlessly links these parts together, resulting in a continuous flow of sophisticated language that captivates and interests your readers.

You go on a journey of refinement and delicacy while refining text through editing and revision. The river becomes your workshop, where you can go over every word, sentence, and paragraph. Each edit, like tributaries merging into the main channel, adds a layer of clarity and effectiveness to your work, contributing to its ultimate coherence and impact. The stream serves as your guide, urging you to navigate the currents of progress and create a piece of art.

Allow yourself to get carried away by the stream of refining text via editing and revision, and see its transformational power. It becomes the lens through which your work is perceived by readers, letting them to fully immerse themselves in the tale without distraction. Your edits, like the river, cut a way through the landscape of your work, revealing the beauty and strength that lurks within.

The continual, fluid rhythm of editing and revision guarantees that refinement is seamlessly integrated into your work. The river guides you, influencing your language choices, phrase patterns, and story flow. The current transforms into a brush, enabling you to smooth down rough edges, clarify concepts, and improve the readability of your work overall.

You observe how each edit changes the reader's experience as you navigate the river of polished text through editing and revision. Revisions become the key to unlocking your writing's full potential, taking it from excellent to spectacular. The current of editing draws readers further into the tale, helping them to appreciate the precision and workmanship behind your words.

Polishing language through editing and rewriting changes the background of your literary universe, offering a lens through which your tale shines inside the moving river. The refining current becomes the driving force, changing readers' perceptions and emotions and letting them to fully appreciate the beauty and strength of your carefully created text.

Editing and revising writing is like riding a continuous, flowing river of refinement, where the currents of thorough analysis and creative elegance blend harmoniously, becoming a polished and compelling written product. Consider jumping into this river, allowing its currents to gently lead you as you go on a journey to improve your work and raise it to its utmost potential.

You become vividly aware of the power of editing and rewriting as you submit to the flowing river. They become your valued partners, assisting you in peeling back the layers to unveil the actual genius of your work. The river transforms into a transformational arena in which you may immerse yourself in the art of words, structure, and clarity. The current seamlessly links these aspects together, resulting in a continuous flow of sophisticated language that captivates and connects with your readers.

You go on a journey of progress and accuracy while improving text through editing and revision. The river becomes your workshop, where you may scrutinize each word, sentence, and paragraph. Each edit, like tributaries merging into the main channel, adds a layer of polish and effectiveness to your work, contributing to its ultimate coherence and impact. The stream becomes your guide, helping you to navigate the currents of refining and create a literary work of art.

Allow yourself to get carried away by the stream of refining text via editing and revision, and see its transformational power. It becomes the prism through which readers experience your work, allowing them to get totally immersed in the tale without distraction. Your edits, like the river, cut a way through the landscape of your work, revealing the beauty and strength that lurks within.

The continual, fluid rhythm of editing and revision guarantees that refinement is seamlessly integrated into your work. The river becomes a guiding force in your writing, influencing your language choices, sentence patterns, and narrative flow. The current transforms into a brush, enabling you to smooth down rough edges, clarify concepts, and improve the readability of your work overall.

You observe how each edit changes the reader's experience as you navigate the river of polished text through editing and revision. Revisions become the key to unlocking your writing's full potential, upgrading it from decent to great. The current of editing draws readers further into the tale, helping them to appreciate the precision and workmanship behind your words.

Polishing language through editing and rewriting changes the background of your literary universe, offering a lens through which your tale shines inside the moving river. The stream of refining becomes the driving force, changing readers' perceptions and emotions so that they may completely appreciate the beauty and power of your well crafted words.

Editing and revising writing is like riding a continuous, flowing river of refinement, where the currents of thorough scrutiny and creative elegance mix smoothly, becoming a polished and compelling written product. Imagine yourself immersed in this river, its currents gently guiding you as you go on a journey to polish your work and raise it to its utmost potential.

You become vividly aware of the power of editing and rewriting as you submit to the flowing river. They become your loyal partners, helping you to smooth out any rough edges and expose the actual brilliance of your work. The river transforms into a place of metamorphosis, where you may become immersed in the complexities of language, structure, and clarity. The current seamlessly links these aspects together, resulting in a continuous flow of sophisticated language that captivates and connects with your readers.

You go on a journey of progress and accuracy while improving text through editing and revision. The river becomes your workplace, a place where you may study each word, sentence, and paragraph with care. Each edit, like tributaries merging into the main channel, adds a layer of polish and effectiveness to your work, contributing to its ultimate coherence and impact. The stream becomes your guide, helping you to navigate the currents of refining and create a literary masterpiece.

Allow yourself to get carried away by the stream of refining text via editing and revision, and see its transformational power. It becomes the prism through which readers experience your work, allowing them to get totally immersed in the tale without distraction. Your edits, like the river, cut a way through the landscape of your work, revealing the beauty and strength that lay within.

The continual, fluid rhythm of editing and revision guarantees that refinement is seamlessly integrated into your work. The river becomes a guiding force in your writing, influencing your language choices, sentence patterns, and narrative flow. The current transforms into a brush, enabling you to smooth down rough edges, clarify concepts, and improve the readability of your work overall.

You observe how each edit changes the reader's experience as you navigate the river of polished text through editing and revision. Revisions become the key to unlocking your writing's full potential, upgrading it from decent to great. The current of editing draws readers further into the tale, helping them to appreciate the precision and workmanship behind your words.

Polishing language through editing and rewriting changes the background of your literary universe, offering a lens through which your tale shines inside the moving river. The stream of refining becomes the driving force, changing readers' perceptions and emotions so that they may completely appreciate the beauty and power of your well crafted words.

Accept the skill of refining language via editing and revision, and allow the river to transport you on a transforming creative trip. Surrender to the process's flexibility, allowing it to mold and improve your words while retaining your own voice. Allow the river of your edits to enchant your readers, encouraging them to immerse themselves in a smooth and polished reading experience that resonates with the strength, clarity, and brilliance of a well-crafted work of literature.

Chapter 8: Writing Engaging Dialogue

Capturing Natural Speech Patterns

Capturing natural speech patterns is similar to navigating a continuous, flowing river of linguistic authenticity, where the currents of dialogue and rhythm blend effortlessly, producing a written work that seems alive and real. Consider immersing yourself in this river, allowing its currents to sweep you along while you try to recreate the intricacies and cadences of spoken language.

You become vividly aware of the power of studying and duplicating natural speech patterns as you succumb to the flowing river. The river transforms into a place of communication and vocal expression, where you may become immersed in the ebb and flow of discussions, pauses and hesitations, and distinctive twists of phrase. The current seamlessly links these aspects together, resulting in a continuous flow of speech that resonates with authenticity and realism.

You go on a voyage of observation and thought while capturing real speech patterns. The river becomes your practice ground, a location where you pay close attention to how people talk, the cadence of their sentences, and the quirks of their distinctive voices. Each discussion, like tributaries merging into the main channel, provides a layer of authenticity, contributing to the overall plausibility and relatability of your characters' discourse. The stream becomes your guide, leading you to traverse the currents of true expression and infuse the authenticity of spoken language into your work.

Allow yourself to get carried away by the tide of recording natural speech patterns and observe its transformational potential. It becomes the prism through which your characters are perceived by readers, allowing them to connect with their conversation on a truly personal level. Your attention to natural speech patterns, like the river, carves a route through your tale, revealing the depth and authenticity of your characters' voices.

The constant, flowing rhythm of recording genuine speech patterns means that realistic dialogue is seamlessly integrated into your writing. The river guides your linguistic choices, sentence constructions, and conversational dynamics. The current transforms into a brush, allowing you to paint fluid dialogues that capture the intricacies of inflection, pace, and tone.

You note how each conversation exchange changes the reader's experience as you navigate the river of capturing real speech patterns. The uttered words become a gateway into your characters' brains and hearts, exposing their emotions, desires, and distinct personalities. The river of real speech envelops readers, dragging them deeper into the story and allowing them to connect with the characters and their true voices.

Capturing genuine speech patterns inside the flowing river defines the backdrop of your literary universe, offering a lens through which your tale evolves. The current of authentic expression becomes the driving force, moulding readers' perceptions and emotions so that they can completely grasp the depth and complexity of your characters' dialogue.

Natural speech patterns are captured by flowing along a continuous, meandering river of linguistic authenticity, where the currents of dialogue and rhythm smoothly blend, producing a written work that seems alive and real. Consider immersing yourself in this river, letting its currents take you along as you try to recreate the intricacies and cadences of spoken language.

You become vividly aware of the power of studying and duplicating natural speech patterns as you succumb to the flowing river. The river transforms into a place of communication and vocal expression, where you may become immersed in the ebb and flow of discussions, pauses and hesitations, and distinctive twists of phrase. The current seamlessly links these aspects together, resulting in a continuous flow of speech that resonates with authenticity and realism.

You go on a voyage of careful observation and thought within the flow of recording real speech patterns. The river becomes your practice ground, a location where you pay close attention to how others talk, absorbing the rhythm of their words and the nuances of their distinctive voices. Each discussion, like tributaries merging into the main channel, provides a layer of authenticity, contributing to the overall plausibility and relatability of your characters' discourse. The stream becomes your guide, leading you to traverse the currents of true expression and infuse the authenticity of spoken language into your work.

Allow yourself to get carried away by the tide of recording natural speech patterns and observe its transformational potential. It becomes the prism through which your characters are perceived by readers, allowing them to connect with their conversation on a truly personal level. Your attention to natural speech patterns, like the river, carves a route through your tale, revealing the depth and authenticity of your characters' voices.

The constant, flowing rhythm of recording genuine speech patterns means that realistic dialogue is seamlessly integrated into your writing. The river guides your linguistic choices, sentence constructions, and conversational dynamics. The current transforms into a brush, allowing you to paint fluid dialogues that capture the intricacies of inflection, pace, and tone.

You note how each conversation exchange changes the reader's experience as you navigate the river of capturing real speech patterns. The uttered words become a gateway into your characters' brains and hearts, exposing their emotions, desires, and distinct personalities. The river of real speech envelops readers, dragging them deeper into the story and allowing them to connect with the characters and their true voices.

Capturing genuine speech patterns inside the flowing river defines the backdrop of your literary universe, offering a lens through which your tale evolves. The current of authentic expression becomes the driving force, moulding readers' perceptions and emotions so that they can completely grasp the depth and complexity of your characters' dialogue.

Capturing genuine speech patterns is like being swept along by a continuous, flowing river of linguistic authenticity, where the currents of dialogue and rhythm mix smoothly, producing a written work that is alive and authentic. Consider surrendering to this river, allowing its currents to gently guide you along as you go on a quest to capture the rich cadences and intricacies of spoken language.

You become vividly aware of the power of sharp observation and painstaking attention to detail as you embrace the rushing river. The river morphs into a domain of communication and vocal expression, immersing you in the ebb and flow of conversations—the pauses, hesitations, and individual phrases. The current seamlessly ties these aspects together, resulting in a continuous stream of discussion that resonates with the true spirit of human communication.

You go on a mission to discover the complexities of how individuals communicate while capturing genuine speech patterns. The river becomes your practice field, where you listen closely to the spoken word, absorbing the rhythms, patterns, and quirks of unique voices. Each interaction, like tributaries merging into the main channel, provides a layer of realism, increasing the overall plausibility and relatability of your characters' communication. The stream serves as your guide, guiding you through the currents of authentic expression and infusing your work with the organic flow of spoken language.

Allow yourself to get carried away by the tide of recording natural speech patterns and observe its transformational potential. It becomes the prism through which your characters are perceived by readers, helping them to form a deep relationship with their voices. Your attention to natural speech patterns, like the river, carves a route through your tale, revealing the depth and authenticity of your characters' voices.

The constant, flowing rhythm of recording genuine speech patterns means that realistic dialogue is seamlessly integrated into your writing. The river guides your linguistic choices, sentence constructions, and conversational dynamics. The current transforms into a brush, allowing you to paint fluid dialogues that capture the intricacies of inflection, intonation, and emotion.

You note how each conversation exchange influences the reader's experience as you navigate the river of capturing real speech patterns. The uttered words become gateways into your characters' hearts and thoughts, exposing their emotions, motives, and distinct personalities. The river of real speech envelops readers, bringing them deeper into the story and developing an intimate relationship with the characters and their genuine voices.

Capturing natural speech patterns inside the flowing river changes the geography of your literary universe, offering a lens through which your tale evolves. The current of authentic expression becomes the driving force, moulding readers' perceptions and emotions so that they can completely grasp the depth and complexity of your characters' dialogue.

Accept the skill of recording natural speech patterns and let the river to lead you on a profound creative voyage. Allow the fluidity of observation and immersion to create and polish your characters' voices while recognizing their uniqueness. Allow your readers to be captivated by the river of true conversation, encouraging them to immerse themselves in a continuous, flowing torrent of words that resound with the strength, authenticity, and relatability of actual spoken language.

Conveying Subtext and Emotion through Dialogue

Subtext and emotion are conveyed through conversation in a continuous, flowing river of hidden depths, where the currents of unspoken meaning and underlying emotions mix fluidly, forming a literary work that resonates with nuance and depth. Consider submitting to this river, allowing its currents to gently carry you along as you go on a journey to reveal the unspoken and elicit tremendous emotions via the words of your characters.

You become fully aware of the power of delicate expression and understated words as you embrace the flowing river. The river becomes a domain of unsaid ideas and unspoken wants, with currents that flow deep with buried meanings and layers of emotion. The river seamlessly ties these parts together, resulting in a constant stream of communication that carries the weight of unsaid ideas and connections.

You go on a mission to comprehend the unwritten language of the human experience via the fluidity of transmitting subtext and emotion through discourse. The river becomes your practice ground, a location where you pay close attention to nonverbal clues, pauses, silences, and the subtextual dance that occurs under the surface of spoken words. Each conversation exchange, like tributaries merging into the main channel, adds a layer of depth and complexity, improving the overall emotional impact of your characters' interactions. The stream becomes your guide, guiding you through the currents of hidden emotions and infusing your writing with the unsaid undercurrents that add richness to your story.

Allow yourself to be carried along by the tide of transmitting subtext and emotion via dialogue and observe its transformational power. It becomes the prism through which your characters' unspoken depths are seen, letting readers to connect with the unsaid and uncover the layers of emotion behind the surface. Your attention to subtext, like the river, carves a course through your tale, revealing the layers and emotional complexity that lie behind the spoken word.

The constant, flowing rhythm of communicating subtext and emotion through conversation guarantees that hidden meaning and emotional resonance are seamlessly integrated into your work. The river guides your linguistic choices, sentence constructions, and conversational dynamics. The current transforms into a brush, allowing you to paint discussions with the weight of unspoken emotions, the strength of unstated desires, and the richness of subtext.

You observe how each interaction changes the reader's experience as you navigate the river of expressing subtext and emotion through conversation. Unspoken words serve as a portal into your characters' inner worlds, revealing their anxieties, longings, and vulnerabilities. Readers are drawn deeper into the story by the stream of subtext, helping them to connect with the unsaid and sense the emotional undercurrents that define your characters' journeys.

Conveying subtext and emotion via conversation alters the landscape of your literary universe, acting as a lens through which your tale evolves. The stream of unspoken meaning becomes the driving force, changing readers' perceptions and emotions and helping them to fully comprehend the complexity and depth of your characters' experiences.

Subtext and emotion are conveyed through conversation in a continuous, flowing river of unspoken meaning, where the currents of underlying emotions and unsaid thoughts blend fluidly, forming a written work that brims with depth and resonance. Consider submitting to the currents of this river as you begin on a trip to reveal the hidden layers of your characters' words and elicit tremendous emotions in your viewers.

You become intensely aware of the force of subtext and the depth of unexpressed emotions as you immerse yourself in the moving river. The river becomes a domain where words carry more than their literal weight, where the currents are rife with unsaid wants, anxieties, and conflicts. The current seamlessly knits these pieces together, resulting in a continuous stream of communication that carries the weight of unspoken ideas and unexpressed connections.

You go on a mission to grasp the unwritten language of human connection within the fluidity of transmitting subtext and emotion through discourse. The river becomes your training field, a place where you can finely study nonverbal signs, pauses laden with meaning, and hidden intents that lay beyond the surface of spoken words. Each interchange, like tributaries merging into the main channel, adds a layer of intricacy to the overall emotional impact of your characters' relationships. The stream serves as your guide, guiding you through the currents of unspoken emotions and infusing your writing with the hidden depths that bring your story to life.

Allow yourself to be carried along by the tide of transmitting subtext and emotion via dialogue and observe its transformational power. It serves as a prism through which readers observe the unsaid layers of your characters' thoughts and feelings, allowing them to connect profoundly with the unsaid and untangle the complexities of their emotions. Your attention to subtext, like the river, carves a course through your narrative, revealing the dense network of unsaid intents and emotional subtleties that lay behind the spoken word.

The constant, flowing rhythm of communicating subtext and emotion through conversation guarantees that hidden meaning and emotional resonance are seamlessly integrated into your work. The river guides your linguistic choices, sentence constructions, and conversational dynamics. The current transforms into a brush, allowing you to paint discussions with the weight of unsaid emotions, the force of unspoken wants, and the depth of unshared weaknesses.

You observe how each interaction changes the reader's experience as you navigate the river of expressing subtext and emotion through conversation. Unspoken words become portals into your characters' inner lives, revealing their secrets, struggles, and longings. Readers are drawn deeper into the story by the stream of subtext, helping them to connect with the unsaid and sense the emotional undercurrents that define your characters' journeys.

Conveying subtext and emotion via conversation alters the landscape of your literary universe, acting as a lens through which your tale evolves. Unspoken meaning becomes the driving force, changing readers' thoughts and emotions and letting them to fully comprehend the complexities and complexity of your characters' experiences.

Subtext and emotion are conveyed through conversation in a continuous, flowing river of unsaid depth, where the currents of hidden meaning and underlying sentiments mix effortlessly, forming a literary work that resonates with subtle complexity. Consider submitting to this river, allowing its currents to gently guide you as you begin on a trip to reveal the unsaid layers underneath your characters' words and elicit tremendous emotions in your readers.

You become intensely aware of the power of subtle hints and unspoken feelings as you immerse yourself in the moving river. The river evolves into a domain where words have more meaning than their surface worth, where currents carry the weight of unspoken desires, unsolved conflicts, and unspoken weaknesses. The current seamlessly links these pieces together, providing a continuous stream of communication with unsaid thoughts and emotional undercurrents.

You go on a mission to grasp the language of silent communication inside the fluidity of communicating subtext and emotion through discourse. The river becomes your training field, a place where you can pay close attention to the intricacies of nonverbal indications, pregnant pauses, and wordless interactions that bring your characters to life. Each conversation exchange, like tributaries merging into the main channel, adds a layer of depth, improving the overall emotional impact of your characters' interactions. The stream becomes your guide, guiding you through the currents of unsaid emotions and infusing your work with the unspoken tapestry that gives your story credibility.

Allow yourself to be carried along by the tide of transmitting subtext and emotion via dialogue and observe its transformational power. It becomes the prism through which your characters' unspoken thoughts and feelings are seen by readers, letting them to connect intimately with the unsaid and untangle the complicated web of their emotions. Your attention to subtext, like the river, carves a course through your narrative, revealing the layers of unsaid intents and emotional depth that lie under the surface of words.

The constant, flowing rhythm of communicating subtext and emotion through conversation guarantees that hidden meaning and emotional resonance are seamlessly integrated into your work. The river guides your linguistic choices, sentence constructions, and conversational dynamics. The current transforms into a brush, allowing you to paint talks with the weight of unspoken wants, the richness of unspoken conflicts, and the rawness of unshared weaknesses.

You observe how each interaction changes the reader's experience as you navigate the river of expressing subtext and emotion through conversation. Unspoken words become gateways into your characters' inner worlds, exposing their secrets, motivations, and emotional intricacies. Readers are drawn deeper into the story by the stream of subtext, helping them to connect with the unsaid and sense the emotional undercurrents that define your characters' journeys.

Conveying subtext and emotion via conversation alters the landscape of your literary universe, acting as a lens through which your tale evolves. Unspoken meaning becomes the driving force, changing readers' thoughts and emotions and letting them to fully comprehend the complexities and complexity of your characters' experiences.

Accept the skill of communicating subtext and emotion via speech, and let the flowing river to take you on a transforming creative trip. Allow the flexibility of observation and interpretation to develop and polish your characters' voices while revealing the unseen layers of emotions. Allow your readers to be captivated by the river of unexpressed depth, encouraging them to immerse themselves in a continuous, flowing torrent of words that resonate with the power, complexity, and emotional depth of true human connection.

Balancing Dialogue with Narrative Description

Balancing conversation with narrative description is like navigating a continuous, flowing river of storytelling, where the currents of character interaction and descriptive language effortlessly blend, forming a written work with a harmonic rhythm and that interests readers on several levels. Imagine surrendering to this river, allowing its currents to gently take you on a trip to find the exact balance between spoken words and vivid story.

As you immerse yourself in the flowing river, you become painfully aware of the power of speech to bring characters to life, as well as the value of descriptive details in creating a rich and immersive universe. The river becomes a world of discourse and imagery, where you must carefully balance what is said and what is seen, ensuring that both components operate in tandem to attract your readers.

You go on a mission to find the perfect combination of interpersonal interaction and atmosphere portrayal within the flexibility of balancing speech with narrative description. The river becomes your practice ground, a place where you pay close attention to the flow of discussion and the sensory nuances that bring your surroundings to life. Each conversation exchange and descriptive passage, like tributaries merging into the main channel, adds depth and complexity to your narrative, increasing the reader's experience. The stream guides you through the currents of engaging conversation and vivid description, moulding your writing into a continuous flow that keeps readers involved in the tale.

Allow yourself to be carried along by the stream of balancing discussion with narrative description and observe its transformational force. It becomes the prism through which readers view the interactions of your characters and picture the world you've built. Your attention to balance carves a way through your tale, revealing the beauty and resonance of both spoken words and descriptive language, just as the river carves a path through the environment.

The constant, fluid rhythm of combining conversation with narrative description guarantees that both aspects are seamlessly integrated into your work. The river becomes your guide, influencing your vocabulary, tempo, and tone. The current transforms into a brush, enabling you to paint discussions that provide insights into the personalities and relationships of your characters, while also employing descriptive elements to create bright and engaging landscapes.

You observe how each conversation changes the reader's experience as you navigate the river of balancing dialogue with narrative description. The conversation becomes your characters' heartbeat, transmitting their thoughts, feelings, and conflicts, while the descriptive sections build a vibrant backdrop, immersing readers in a sensory experience. The current of balance envelops readers, dragging them further into the story and allowing them to connect intellectually as well as viscerally.

Balanced conversation and narrative description build the environment of your literary universe, offering a lens through which your story evolves. The equilibrium current becomes the driving force, changing readers' perceptions and emotions and helping them to fully comprehend the richness and complexity of your characters' experiences.

Balancing conversation with narrative description is similar to navigating a continuous, flowing river of storytelling, where the currents of character interaction and vivid writing blend smoothly, forming a written work that dances between spoken words and descriptive passages. Consider submitting to this river, allowing its currents to gently guide you as you go on a journey to achieve a healthy balance between your characters' voices and the vivid world they occupy.

As you become immersed in the rushing river, you become painfully aware of the delicate dance between speech and description, each of which plays an important part in captivating readers and immersing them in the tale. The river becomes a tapestry of discussions and sensory imagery, and you must carefully control the balance to ensure that neither aspect overpowers the other, but rather flows in perfect harmony.

You go on a mission to locate the sweet spot where character voices come alive through spoken words and the surroundings are painted with brilliant strokes of descriptive writing within the flow of mixing conversation with narrative description. The river becomes your practice ground, a place where you pay close attention to the rhythms of dialogue and the rich nuances that make the world come alive. Each conversation exchange and descriptive paragraph, like tributaries flowing into the main channel, adds depth, texture, and a feeling of location to the fabric of the tale. The stream serves as your guide, guiding you through the currents of fascinating conversation and engrossing description, maintaining a consistent flow that captivates readers from beginning to end.

Allow yourself to be carried along by the stream of balancing discussion with narrative description and observe its transformational force. It becomes the prism through which readers see your characters' life and the universe in which they exist. Your attention to balance, like the river, carves a way through your tale, revealing the beauty and resonance of both spoken words and the vivid fabric of the world.

The constant, fluid rhythm of combining conversation with narrative description guarantees that both aspects are seamlessly integrated into your work. The river guides you, defining the rhythm, tone, and atmosphere. The current transforms into a brush, enabling you to design dialogues that expose your characters' thoughts, feelings, and dynamics, while also employing descriptive elements to create a vibrant backdrop that takes readers to the heart of the tale.

You observe how each exchange and description affects the reader's experience as you navigate the river of balancing conversation with narrative description. The speech brings your characters to life by giving them realistic and emotional voices. The descriptive sections provide a visual and sensual feast for readers, immersing them in the world you've created. The current of balance envelops readers, dragging them further into the story and allowing them to interact with it on various levels.

Balanced conversation and narrative description build the environment of your literary universe, offering a lens through which your story evolves. The equilibrium current becomes the driving force, changing readers' perceptions and emotions and helping them to fully comprehend the richness and complexity of your characters' experiences.

Balancing conversation with narrative description is like skillfully navigating a continuous, flowing river of storytelling, where the currents of character interaction and brilliant prose mingle perfectly, resulting in a written work that seamlessly integrates spoken words with vivid descriptions. Imagine yourself succumbing to the gentle guiding of this river as it takes you on a mesmerizing trip to create the right balance between conversation and descriptive sections.

Immersing yourself in the flowing river sharpens your sensitivity to the subtle dance of dialogue and description, understanding their distinct roles in capturing readers and immersing them in the narrative fabric. The river develops into a mesmerizing universe where talks coexist with evocative images, and you manage its currents with extreme caution, establishing a healthy balance in which neither aspect overshadows the other but instead intertwines seamlessly.

You go on a mission to harness the power of character voices and infuse life into the environment they live within the fluidity of mixing dialogue with narrative description. The river becomes your practice ground, a place where you carefully watch the ebb and flow of dialogue, as well as the bright details that bring your settings to life. Each conversation exchange and descriptive passage, like tributaries merging into the main channel, adds to the fabric of the tale, providing it with depth, texture, and a distinct feeling of location. You navigate the currents of fascinating conversation and engrossing description, guided by the stream, keeping a continuous flow that captivates readers from beginning to end.

You bore witness to the transformational force of the current of balancing discussion with narrative description. It becomes the prism through which readers see your characters' life and the universe in which they exist. Your attention to balance, like the river, carves a way through your tale, excavating the beauty and resonance of both spoken words and the colorful tapestry of the world surrounding your characters.

The constant, fluid rhythm of combining conversation with narrative description guarantees that both aspects are seamlessly integrated into your work. The river becomes your guide, determining the narrative's speed, tone, and feel. Its current transforms into a brush, allowing you to deftly weave conversations that expose your characters' inner thoughts, feelings, and dynamics, while descriptive sections paint vivid backgrounds that take readers into the heart of the tale.

You see how each interaction and description affects the reader's experience as you navigate the river of balancing conversation with narrative description. The conversation brings your characters to life by giving them real voices that are full of emotion and authenticity. The vivid paragraphs elicit a sensory feast, immersing readers in your beautifully built world's sights, sounds, and experiences. Readers are lured further into the tale, engaging their senses and emotions at the same time, as they become submerged in the stream of balance.

Balancing conversation and narrative description inside the flowing river changes the entire topography of your literary universe, offering a lens through which your story naturally unfolds. The equilibrium current becomes the driving force, changing readers' perceptions and emotions and helping them to fully comprehend the richness, depth, and complexity of your characters' experiences.

Accept the challenge of blending dialogue with narrative description, and let the flowing river to transport you on a transforming creative trip. Allow the fluidity of observation and refinement to mold and polish your characters' voices as well as create evocative environments that transport readers. Allow your readers to be captivated by the river of balanced storytelling, encouraging them to immerse themselves in a continuous, flowing torrent of words that resonates with the strength, authenticity, and immersive characteristics of a brilliant tale.

Chapter 9: Managing Time and Pacing

Controlling Narrative Tempo

Controlling narrative pace is like navigating a continuous, flowing river of storytelling, where the currents of pacing and rhythm blend harmoniously, producing a written work that takes readers on an immersive trip. Consider succumbing to the soothing guiding of this river as it carries you through the ebb and flow of your tale, enabling you to choose the speed and intensity of the storytelling experience.

Immerse yourself in the flowing river, and you'll get an understanding of the power of narrative tempo, the art of modulating the pace and rhythm of your writing to elicit certain emotions and connect readers on a deeper level. The river develops into a dynamic environment, with shifting currents and swaying trees, and you manage its waters with precision, controlling the ebb and flow to produce a constant stream of storytelling that captivates your audience.

You engage on a journey to balance moments of tension and release, acceleration and deceleration, precisely as the currents of the river that carry you along, within the fluidity of managing narrative tempo. The river becomes your practice ground, a place where you carefully notice the beats and pauses, the narrative's acceleration and deceleration. Each scene, sentence, and word, like tributaries merging into the main channel, contributes to the overall speed of your writing, forming the emotional experience for your readers. You manage the currents of tempo and rhythm, guided by the stream, to create a continuous flow that keeps readers interested and hungry for more.

Surrendering to the tide of narrative pace control, you experience its transformational force. It takes on the role of conductor of emotions, arranging the highs and lows, frantic thrill and contemplative thought. Your attention to pace carves a channel through your narrative, revealing the symphony of emotions that resonate with readers, just as the river carves a way through the landscape.

The continuous, flowing rhythm of regulating narrative pace guarantees that tension and release, acceleration and slowdown, are seamlessly integrated into your work. The river becomes your guide, creating the narrative's energy's rise and fall. Its current acts as a metronome, letting you to fine-tune the rhythm, heightening suspense or settling into silent contemplation.

You can see how each twist and turn, each rise and fall, effects the reader's experience as you navigate the river of regulating narrative speed. The pace establishes the tone, pushes the action, and amplifies the emotional effect. Readers are lured deeper into the tale by the current of pace, their hearts racing or their thoughts appreciating the peaceful moments, echoing the rhythm you have painstakingly established.

Controlling narrative pace influences the actual topography of your literary universe within the flowing river, offering a lens through which your story evolves. The cadence of the story becomes the driving force, molding readers' expectations and emotional responses and helping them to fully enjoy the experience you've created for them.

Controlling narrative pace is analogous to skillfully navigating a continuous, flowing river of storytelling, where the currents of pacing and rhythm blend flawlessly, resulting in a written work that captivates and totally immerses readers in the narrative trip. Consider succumbing to the gentle guiding of this river as it sweeps you down its meandering route, enabling you to choose the speed and intensity of the storytelling experience.

Immerse yourself in the flowing river, and you'll become sensitive to the power of narrative tempo—the skill of regulating the ebb and flow of the story's speed and rhythm to elicit certain emotions and improve the overall reading experience. The river becomes a dynamic conduit, with currents that shift and swing, and you navigate its waters with elegance, masterfully harnessing the ebb and flow to generate a constant stream of storytelling that captivates and engages your audience.

You go on a mission to perfect the balance between moments of tension and release, acceleration and deceleration, exactly as the currents of the river lead your trip. The river becomes your practice ground, a place where you pay close attention to the beats and pauses, the periods of heightened exhilaration and quieter introspection. Each scene, paragraph, and phrase, like tributaries merging into the main river, contributes to the overall speed of your writing, determining the emotional impact on your readers. You effectively handle the currents of tempo and rhythm, generating a continuous flow that keeps readers interested and wanting to flip the page, guided by the stream.

Surrendering to the tide of narrative pace control, you experience its transformational force. It takes on the role of conductor of emotions, orchestrating the ups and downs, peaks and valleys that define the narrative landscape. Your attention to pace, like the river, carves a route through your tale, revealing the symphony of emotions that connects with readers and elicits a visceral response.

The constant, flowing rhythm of regulating narrative tempo guarantees that periods of tension and anticipation, excitement and tranquility, are seamlessly integrated into your work. The river becomes your guide, dictating the story's rise and fall of energy and tension. Its current becomes a metronome, allowing you to regulate the tempo with deftness, heightening climax moments or lowering the narrative pace to build anticipation.

You can see how each twist and turn, each shift in speed, affects the reader's experience as you navigate the river of manipulating narrative tempo. The pace establishes the mood, pushes the action, and promotes emotional involvement. Readers are lured deeper into the tale by the current of tempo, their hearts racing or their thoughts absorbing the quieter parts, echoing the rhythm you have painstakingly established.

Controlling narrative pace changes the actual topography of your literary universe within the flowing river, offering a lens through which your story smoothly unfolds. The tempo current becomes the driving force, guiding readers' expectations and emotional responses and letting them to fully comprehend the complexities of your narrative journey.

Controlling narrative pace is like to expertly navigating a continuous, flowing river of storytelling, where the currents of pacing and rhythm mix flawlessly, producing a written work that interests and captivates readers from beginning to finish. Consider yourself submitting to the soothing stream of the river as it sweeps you through the twists and turns of your story, enabling you to choose the speed and intensity to create an immersive reading experience.

Immerse yourself in the river, and you'll learn the art of manipulating narrative tempo—the capacity to change the speed and rhythm of your writing to elicit certain emotions, heighten suspense, or provide moments of rest. The river takes on a life of its own, with its currents mirroring the varied speeds and intensities of your narration. You take on the role of navigator, expertly harnessing these currents to create a continuous flow that keeps readers interested and anxious to find out what comes next.

You go on a journey to achieve the correct balance between momentum and pause, accelerating and decelerating as the tale requires, within the flexibility of managing narrative pace. The river serves as a training ground for you, a place where you can closely examine the ebb and flow of the narrative's energy. Each scene, paragraph, and phrase, like tributaries merging into the main channel, contributes to the overall speed of your writing, influencing the reading experience. You traverse the currents of tempo and rhythm, guided by the stream, to create a seamless flow that leads readers through the narrative's arc.

Surrendering to the tide of narrative pace control, you experience its transformational force. It takes on the role of conductor, directing the rise and fall, the times of tension and release, as if writing a symphony that connects with the emotions of the readers. Your attention to pace carves a way through your narrative, revealing the rhythm that immerses readers in the story, just as the river carves a path through the environment.

Controlling narrative pacing in a continuous, flowing rhythm provides a harmonic combination of fast-paced periods and thoughtful pauses, moving the story ahead while enabling readers to breathe and absorb the unfolding events. The river becomes your guide, affecting the story's rise and fall of energy. Its current acts as a metronome, letting you to control the tempo, speeding at exciting and suspenseful periods or slowing down to explore introspection and reflection.

You can see how each adjustment in rhythm, each modification in speed, effects the reader's experience as you navigate the river of controlling narrative tempo. The pace establishes the mood, heightening anticipation, amplifying emotions, or providing rest in calmer interludes. Readers are lured deeper into the tale by the current of pace, their heartbeat racing or their thoughts thoughtful, echoing the rhythm you have painstakingly established.

Controlling narrative pace influences the actual topography of your literary universe within the flowing river, offering a lens through which your story evolves. The cadence of the story becomes the driving force, molding readers' involvement and emotional connection and helping them to fully immerse themselves in the developing narrative.

Accept the skill of regulating narrative tempo and allow the flowing river to take you on a transforming creative trip. Allow the flexibility of tempo and rhythm to form and develop the emotional effect of your tale. Allow your readers to be captivated by the river of controlled pace, encouraging them to delve into a continuous, flowing torrent of words that resonates with the strength, authenticity, and immersive aspects of a brilliant tale.

Balancing Action and Reflection

Balancing action and introspection is like to navigating a continuous, flowing river of storytelling, where the currents of dramatic events and reflective moments blend harmoniously, forming a written work that interests readers on several levels. Consider submitting to the soothing stream of this river as it sweeps you through the lively action scenes and peaceful contemplation, allowing you to reach the right balance between the two.

When you immerse yourself in the rushing river, you'll find the art of balancing activity and reflection—the capacity to integrate periods of intense movement and outward events with deliberate meditation and interior investigation. The river transforms into a living canvas, with its currents symbolizing the energy and movement of your tale. You take on the role of navigator, expertly harnessing these currents to produce a continuous flow that keeps readers engaged in the plot's twists and turns.

You go on a quest to find the optimal equilibrium between moments of exhilaration and periods of meditation within the fluidity of balancing activity and reflection. The river becomes your practice ground, a place where you pay close attention to the interaction of external occurrences and interior ideas. Each action-packed scene and contemplative piece, like tributaries converging into the main river, contributes to the overall balance of your writing, providing readers with a complete experience. You travel the currents of action and contemplation, guided by the stream, producing a seamless flow that allows readers to simultaneously witness the events and enter into the characters' inner lives.

You observe the transformational force of the stream of balanced action and meditation when you surrender to it. It becomes the conduit that connects the exterior and interior worlds, weaving a complex tapestry of experiences together. Your attention to balance carves a way through your tale, revealing the intricacy and depth of your characters and their journey, just as the river does.

The fluid rhythm of action and thought provides a smooth combination of energetic occurrences and contemplative pauses. The river becomes your guide, affecting the story's rise and fall of energy. Its current acts as a conductor, enabling you to set your own rhythm, alternating between explosive action passages and peaceful periods of introspection.

You can see how each movement in emphasis, each transition between activity and introspection, influences the reader's experience as you navigate the river of balancing action and reflection. The balance establishes the tone, bringing excitement, suspense, and external conflict while allowing for character development, emotional depth, and personal progress. Readers get completely absorbed in the flow of the narrative, their hearts pumping during action-packed passages and their brains engaged during periods of contemplation, echoing the rhythm you've painstakingly established.

Balancing movement and meditation inside the flowing river creates the entire geography of your literary universe, offering a lens through which your tale evolves. The current of balance becomes the driving force, molding readers' involvement and emotional connection and helping them to fully comprehend your characters and their journey.

Balancing action and introspection is like smoothly navigating a continuous, flowing river of storytelling, where the currents of dramatic events and contemplative moments mix harmoniously, producing a written work that captivates readers with its depth. Consider submitting to the soothing stream of this river as it transports you on a trip that combines intense action sequences with profound periods of contemplation, resulting in a beautiful blend of outward and internal experiences.

Immerse yourself in the flowing river, and you'll discover the skilful interaction between periods of tremendous intensity and moments of introspection, providing a constant flow that stimulates readers' minds and emotions. The river becomes a dynamic tapestry, with the currents representing the events that move the narrative ahead and the quiet waters allowing characters to dig into their deepest thoughts and feelings. You take on the role of navigator, carefully controlling these currents to create a cohesive narrative that immerses viewers completely in the story.

You go on a mission to find the delicate balance between outward occurrences and inward contemplation within the fluidity of balancing action and introspection. The river serves as your training field, a place where you can closely examine the rise and fall of action-packed scenarios as well as calm periods of meditation. Each action sequence and contemplative piece, like tributaries merging into the main river, contributes to the overall balance of your writing, providing readers with a multi-layered experience. You masterfully control the currents of action and introspection, maintaining a continuous flow that allows readers to see outward occurrences while also exploring the characters' inner lives.

You observe the transformational force of the stream of balanced action and meditation when you surrender to it. It becomes the conduit that smoothly ties together external forces and interior progress, resulting in a very moving story. Your attention to balance carves a way through your tale, revealing the intricacy and depth of your characters' travels, just as the river does.

The fluid rhythm of action and meditation provides a smooth combination of active occurrences and contemplative pauses. The river becomes your guide, determining the story's rise and fall of energy. Its current acts as a conductor, enabling you to set the tempo, alternating between fast-paced action and thoughtful pauses that provide insight into the characters' thoughts, feelings, and evolution.

You can see how each shift in attention, each transition between external and interior, influences the reader's experience as you navigate the river of balancing action and introspection. The tone is determined by the balance, which provides excitement, suspense, and external conflict while also allowing for character development, emotional depth, and self-discovery. Readers get completely absorbed in the flow of the narrative, their pulses racing during exhilarating parts and their brains engaged during periods of meditation, echoing the rhythm you have painstakingly established.

Balancing action and meditation inside the flowing river creates the entire geography of your literary universe, offering a lens through which your tale smoothly evolves. The balancing current becomes the driving force, molding readers' involvement and emotional connection and letting them to fully grasp the multifaceted qualities of your characters and their travels.

Balancing action and introspection is like to navigating a continuous, flowing river of storytelling, where the currents of dramatic events and reflective moments blend harmoniously, forming a written work that interests readers on several levels. Consider submitting to the soothing stream of this river as it sweeps you through the lively action scenes and peaceful contemplation, allowing you to reach the right balance between the two.

When you immerse yourself in the rushing river, you'll find the art of balancing activity and reflection—the capacity to integrate periods of intense movement and outward events with deliberate meditation and interior investigation. The river transforms into a living canvas, with its currents symbolizing the energy and movement of your tale. You take on the role of navigator, expertly harnessing these currents to produce a continuous flow that keeps readers engaged in the plot's twists and turns.

You go on a quest to find the optimal equilibrium between moments of exhilaration and periods of meditation within the fluidity of balancing activity and reflection. The river serves as a training ground for you, a place where you can closely examine the ebb and flow of the narrative's energy. Each action-packed scene and contemplative piece, like tributaries converging into the main river, contributes to the overall balance of your writing, providing readers with a complete experience. You travel the currents of action and contemplation, guided by the stream, producing a seamless flow that allows readers to simultaneously witness the events and enter into the characters' inner lives.

You observe the transformational force of the stream of balanced action and meditation when you surrender to it. It becomes the conduit that connects the exterior and interior worlds, weaving a complex tapestry of experiences together. Your attention to balance carves a way through your tale, revealing the intricacy and depth of your characters and their journey, just as the river does.

The fluid rhythm of action and thought provides a smooth combination of energetic occurrences and contemplative pauses. The river becomes your guide, affecting the story's rise and fall of energy. Its current acts as a conductor, enabling you to set your own rhythm, alternating between explosive action passages and peaceful periods of introspection.

You can see how each movement in emphasis, each transition between activity and introspection, influences the reader's experience as you navigate the river of balancing action and reflection. The balance establishes the tone, bringing excitement, suspense, and external conflict while allowing for character development, emotional depth, and personal progress. Readers get completely absorbed in the flow of the narrative, their hearts pumping during action-packed passages and their brains engaged during periods of contemplation, echoing the rhythm you've painstakingly established.

Balancing movement and meditation inside the flowing river creates the entire geography of your literary universe, offering a lens through which your tale evolves. The current of balance becomes the driving force, molding readers' involvement and emotional connection and helping them to fully comprehend your characters and their journey.

Accept the skill of balancing activity and introspection, and allow the river to lead you on a transforming creative trip. Allow the flexibility of tempo and rhythm to form and develop the emotional effect of your tale. Allow your readers to be captivated by the river of balance, encouraging them to immerse themselves in a continuous, flowing torrent of words that resonates with the power, authenticity, and immersive characteristics of a brilliant tale.

Utilizing Flashbacks and Foreshadowing

Using flashbacks and foreshadowing is like navigating a continuous, flowing river of storytelling, where the currents of past and future harmoniously mix, producing a written work that attracts readers and adds depth to the narrative trip. Consider submitting to the smooth stream of this river as it leads you through the present moment while expertly weaving in views of the past and indications of what is to come.

Immerse yourself in the flowing river, and you'll discover the skill of using flashbacks and foreshadowing—the capacity to transport readers to important moments in the characters' pasts or to provide tantalizing views of events yet to come. The river transforms into a dynamic tapestry, with its currents signifying time and the connectivity of past, present, and future. You take on the role of navigator, expertly navigating these currents to produce a continuous flow that keeps readers captivated and ready to understand the story's intricacies.

You go on a mission to strike the delicate balance between disclosing the past and hinting at the future through the fluidity of using flashbacks and foreshadowing. The river serves as your training field, a place where you may closely study the events that molded your characters' lives as well as the tiny hints that lead to future discoveries. Each flashback and foreshadowing moment, like tributaries merging into the main river, adds to the overall tapestry of your work, providing readers with a rich and multi-dimensional experience. You weave the currents of time, smoothly combining past and future with the present, providing a fluid flow that helps readers to explore the narrative's multiple layers.

You observe the transformational power of memories and foreboding when you surrender to the current. It becomes the link that links the dots, shedding light on the characters' motivations and expanding the reader's comprehension. Your attention to detail carves a way through your narrative, revealing the connectivity of past, present, and future, just as the river carves a path through the environment.

The use of flashbacks and foreshadowing in a continuous, flowing rhythm creates a seamless integration of multiple historical periods, allowing readers to smoothly travel the river of storytelling. The river becomes your guide, determining the rise and fall of the story's chronological transitions. Its current serves as a conduit, allowing you to move between the past, present, and future, providing readers with a multifaceted and deep reading experience.

You can see how each shift in time, each look into the past or future, influences the reader's experience as you navigate the river of using flashbacks and foreshadowing. Flashbacks provide depth and meaning to the story by exposing the characters' backstories and offering insights into their motives. Foreshadowing builds suspense and anticipation by setting the stage for future occurrences. Readers get completely involved in the flow of the narrative, their thoughts fitting together the jigsaw of the story, mimicking the rhythm you have painstakingly established.

Using flashbacks and foreshadowing inside the flowing river alters the entire topography of your literary universe, offering a lens through which your tale naturally unfolds. The passage of time becomes the driving force, molding readers' involvement and emotional connection and helping them to fully comprehend the intricacy and intricacies of your story.

Using flashbacks and foreshadowing is like navigating a continuous, flowing river of storytelling, where the currents of past and future harmoniously mix, producing a written work that attracts readers and adds depth to the narrative trip. Consider surrendering to the soothing stream of this river as it sweeps you through the present moment while skilfully weaving in views of the past and indications of what is to come.

Immerse yourself in the flowing river, and you'll discover the skill of using flashbacks and foreshadowing—the capacity to transport readers to important moments in the characters' pasts or to provide tantalizing views of events yet to come. The river transforms into a dynamic tapestry, with its currents signifying time and the connectivity of past, present, and future. You take on the role of navigator, expertly navigating these currents to produce a continuous flow that keeps readers captivated and ready to understand the story's intricacies.

You go on a mission to strike the delicate balance between disclosing the past and hinting at the future through the fluidity of using flashbacks and foreshadowing. The river serves as your training field, a place where you may closely study the events that molded your characters' lives as well as the tiny hints that lead to future discoveries. Each flashback and foreshadowing moment, like tributaries merging into the main river, adds to the overall tapestry of your work, providing readers with a rich and multi-dimensional experience. You weave the currents of time, smoothly combining past and future with the present, providing a fluid flow that helps readers to explore the narrative's multiple layers.

You observe the transformational power of memories and foreboding when you surrender to the current. It becomes the link that links the dots, shedding light on the characters' motivations and expanding the reader's comprehension. Your attention to detail carves a way through your narrative, revealing the connectivity of past, present, and future, just as the river carves a path through the environment.

The use of flashbacks and foreshadowing in a continuous, flowing rhythm creates a seamless integration of multiple historical periods, allowing readers to smoothly travel the river of storytelling. The river becomes your guide, determining the rise and fall of the story's chronological transitions. Its current serves as a conduit, allowing you to move between the past, present, and future, providing readers with a multifaceted and deep reading experience.

You can see how each shift in time, each look into the past or future, influences the reader's experience as you navigate the river of using flashbacks and foreshadowing. Flashbacks provide depth and meaning to the story by exposing the characters' backstories and offering insights into their motives. Foreshadowing builds suspense and anticipation by setting the stage for future occurrences. Readers get completely involved in the flow of the narrative, their thoughts fitting together the jigsaw of the story, mimicking the rhythm you have painstakingly established.

Using flashbacks and foreshadowing inside the flowing river alters the entire topography of your literary universe, offering a lens through which your tale naturally unfolds. The passage of time becomes the driving force, molding readers' involvement and emotional connection and helping them to fully comprehend the intricacy and intricacies of your story.

Using flashbacks and foreshadowing in storytelling is like to expertly navigating a continuous, flowing river, where the currents of the past and future blend to create an engaging narrative experience. Consider surrendering to the soothing stream of this river as it transports you through the present while skilfully combining glimpses of the past and indications of what is to come.

Immerse yourself in the flowing river, and you'll discover the skill of using flashbacks and foreshadowing—the capacity to take readers to crucial moments in the characters' pasts or to provide tantalizing views of future events. The river transforms into a dynamic tapestry, with its currents signifying time and the connectivity of the story's aspects. You take on the role of navigator, expertly steering these currents to produce a continuous flow that fascinates readers and piques their interest.

You go on a mission to strike the proper balance between disclosing the past and teasing future events within the fluidity of employing flashbacks and foreshadowing. The river serves as your training field, where you closely notice the events that formed the people' lives as well as the subtle hints that predict what is to come. Each flashback and foreshadowing event becomes a tributary that merges smoothly with the main river of the tale, adding to the broader tapestry of your storytelling. You explore the currents of time, guided by the river's flow, effortlessly combining past, present, and future, producing a unified and interesting reading experience.

You observe the transformational power of memories and foreboding when you surrender to the current. It serves as a link between the story's strands, shedding light on the characters' motives and providing complexity to their travels. Your attention to detail carves a way through your narrative, exposing the interplay between previous experiences and future possibilities, just as the river carves a path through the environment.

The constant, flowing rhythm of using flashbacks and foreshadowing guarantees the story's harmonic integration of numerous time frames. The river becomes your guide, affecting the rise and fall of temporal transitions and providing readers with a smooth voyage across the timeframe of the tale. Its current serves as a conduit, allowing you to easily traverse between the past, present, and future, providing an immersive and multi-dimensional reading experience.

You can see how each shift in time, each look into the past or future, influences the reader's experience as you navigate the river of using flashbacks and foreshadowing. Flashbacks provide us a better knowledge of the characters' pasts, revealing their motives and affecting their current actions. Foreshadowing builds suspense and excitement by laying breadcrumbs that attract readers to discover what comes next. Readers get completely absorbed in the narrative's ebb and flow, their interest peaked and engagement enhanced, echoing the well planned rhythm of your storytelling.

Using flashbacks and foreshadowing inside the flowing river affects the entire environment of your story, offering a lens through which the narrative unfolds. The passage of time acts as a driving force, forming readers' emotional connections and expanding their comprehension of the characters and their travels.

Accept the art of using flashbacks and foreshadowing, and allow the river to lead you on a transforming creative trip. Allow the mobility of time to form and develop the emotional effect of your tale. Allow your readers to be captivated by the river of past and future, encouraging them to immerse themselves in a continuous, flowing torrent of words that resonates with the power, authenticity, and immersive characteristics of a brilliant story.

Chapter 10: Enhancing Writing through Research

Conducting Effective Research for Fiction Writing

Conducting excellent research for fiction writing is like starting on a voyage down a never-ending river of knowledge, where the currents of information blend perfectly with your imagination, forming a rich and real narrative experience. Consider submitting to the smooth stream of this river as it sweeps you through the broad domain of study, revealing the ideas and nuances that bring your fictional world to life.

Immerse yourself in the river's current, and you'll acquire the technique of performing good research for fiction writing—the ability to gather essential material and smoothly integrate it into your tale. The river transforms into a dynamic tapestry, with its currents signifying the huge diversity of materials at your disposal to feed your creativity. You take on the role of explorer, expertly navigating these currents in search of the jewels that will add authenticity and depth to your story.

You go on a mission to strike the right mix between creativity and factual accuracy while performing successful research. The river serves as your guide, providing a multitude of tools to help you realize your creative idea. Each piece of information, like tributaries merging into the main channel, adds to the overall tapestry of your writing, providing readers with a feeling of reality and grounding. You explore the currents of knowledge, guided by the stream, carefully picking and assimilating the facts that will enrich your fictitious universe.

Surrendering to the tide of successful research reveals its transformational potential. It becomes the source of your storytelling, guaranteeing that even the most innovative components of your fiction are grounded in fact. Your attention to detail carves a way through your tale, infusing it with authenticity and depth, just as the river carves a path through the environment.

The continual, flowing rhythm of successful research guarantees that factual knowledge is seamlessly integrated into your narrative. The river becomes a source of inspiration for you, influencing the ups and downs of your creative process. Its current acts as a conduit, allowing you to smoothly traverse between the realms of imagination and reality, resulting in a story that seems both credible and captivating.

As you go down the river of successful research, you'll see how each nugget of information, each dip into the huge sea of knowledge, improves your narrative. Research becomes a tool for creating convincing people, vivid locations, and sophisticated plotlines. It lays the groundwork for your imagination to thrive, providing readers with an engaging and deep reading experience. Readers become completely engaged in the flow of the tale, their interest peaked by the depth of the universe you've constructed, echoing the rhythm you've painstakingly established.

Conducting successful research inside the flowing river affects the entire topography of your literary universe, offering a lens through which your tale evolves. The flow of information becomes the driving force, molding reader engagement and developing their connection to your fictional world.

Conducting good research for fiction writing is analogous to going on a continuous, flowing river of knowledge, where the currents of information seamlessly combine with the creative currents of your imagination. Consider succumbing to the soothing stream of this river as it transports you across a huge expanse of resources and ideas, revealing the intricacies that bring your imaginary world to life.

Immerse yourself in the flowing river, and you'll learn the technique of conducting excellent research for fiction writing—a talent that will allow you to acquire and smoothly incorporate essential material into your stories. The river transforms into a living tapestry, with its currents signifying the great diversity of resources available to you. You take on the role of explorer, expertly navigating these currents in search of knowledge nuggets that will add authenticity and depth to your story.

You go on a mission to create the optimal mix between creativity and factual accuracy while completing excellent research. The river serves as your guide, providing a multitude of tools to help you realize your creative idea. Each piece of research, like tributaries merging into the main river, adds to the overall tapestry of your writing, establishing a foundation of reality that attracts and captivates readers. You travel the currents of knowledge, guided by the stream, carefully picking and weaving together the material that will enhance your fictitious universe.

Surrendering to the tide of successful research reveals its transformational potential. It becomes the source of your tale, guaranteeing that even the most outlandish components of your work are based in truth. Your attention to detail carves a path through your tale, infusing it with depth and authenticity, just as the river carves a way through the environment.

The continual, flowing rhythm of successful research guarantees that factual knowledge is seamlessly integrated into your narrative. The river transforms into your muse, shaping the ups and downs of your creative process. Its current acts as a conduit, allowing you to smoothly traverse between the realms of imagination and reality, resulting in a captivating and realistic tale.

As you go down the river of efficient research, you'll see how each nugget of information, each journey into the huge sea of knowledge, improves your storytelling. Research is used to develop well-rounded characters, create vivid and engaging environments, and generate sophisticated plotlines. It gives the framework for your creativity to thrive, providing readers with a rich and pleasant reading experience. Readers are completely involved in the flow of the tale, their interest peaked by the richness of your world-building, which mirrors the rhythm you have skilfully built.

Conducting successful research inside the flowing river affects the entire topography of your literary universe, offering a lens through which your tale smoothly unfolds. The flow of information becomes the driving force, molding reader engagement and developing their connection to your fictional world.

Conducting good research for fiction writing is analogous to going on a continuous, flowing river of knowledge, where the currents of information seamlessly combine with the creative currents of your imagination. Consider submitting to the smooth stream of this river as it transports you across a huge expanse of resources and ideas, revealing the intricacies that bring your imaginary world to life.

Immerse yourself in the flowing river, and you'll learn the technique of conducting excellent research for fiction writing—a talent that will allow you to acquire and smoothly incorporate essential material into your stories. The river transforms into a living tapestry, with its currents signifying the great diversity of resources available to you. You take on the role of explorer, expertly navigating these currents in search of knowledge nuggets that will add authenticity and depth to your story.

You go on a mission to create the optimal mix between creativity and factual accuracy while completing excellent research. The river serves as your guide, providing a multitude of tools to help you realize your creative idea. Each piece of research, like tributaries merging into the main river, adds to the overall tapestry of your writing, establishing a foundation of reality that attracts and captivates readers. You travel the currents of knowledge, guided by the stream, carefully picking and weaving together the material that will enhance your fictitious universe.

Surrendering to the tide of successful research reveals its transformational potential. It becomes the source of your tale, guaranteeing that even the most outlandish components of your work are based in truth. Your attention to detail carves a path through your tale, infusing it with depth and authenticity, just as the river carves a way through the environment.

The continual, flowing rhythm of successful research guarantees that factual knowledge is seamlessly integrated into your narrative. The river transforms into your muse, shaping the ups and downs of your creative process. Its current acts as a conduit, allowing you to smoothly traverse between the realms of imagination and reality, resulting in a captivating and realistic tale.

As you go down the river of efficient research, you'll see how each nugget of information, each journey into the huge sea of knowledge, improves your storytelling. Research is used to develop well-rounded characters, create vivid and engaging environments, and generate sophisticated plotlines. It gives the framework for your creativity to thrive, providing readers with a rich and pleasant reading experience. Readers are completely involved in the flow of the tale, their interest peaked by the richness of your world-building, which mirrors the rhythm you have skilfully built.

Conducting successful research inside the flowing river affects the entire topography of your literary universe, offering a lens through which your tale smoothly unfolds. The flow of information becomes the driving force, molding reader engagement and developing their connection to your fictional world.

Accept the technique of performing successful research for fiction writing and let the river to transport you on a profound creative voyage. Allow the flow of information to develop and improve the authenticity of your tale. Allow your readers to be captivated by the river of research, encouraging them to immerse themselves in a continuous, flowing torrent of words that resonates with the strength, authenticity, and immersive characteristics of a brilliant story.

Incorporating Real-World Elements and Authenticity

Incorporating real-life aspects and authenticity into your work is akin to blending a continuous, flowing river of reality with the colourful landscape of your fictitious realm. Imagine submitting to this river's soothing current as it leads you through the rich tapestry of the actual world, infusing your work with a sense of reality and resonance.

Immerse yourself in the river, and you'll learn the art of combining real-world elements and authenticity—a talent that allows you to draw on the depth and complexity of reality to improve your narrative. The river transforms into a conduit, connecting you to a huge array of human experiences, civilizations, and surroundings. You become the explorer, expertly navigating these currents to capture the essence of authenticity and effortlessly weave it into your story.

You go on a mission to find the right balance between fantasy and reality by combining real-world components. The river becomes your source of inspiration, providing a plethora of unique events, places, and people. Each real-world aspect, like tributaries merging into the main channel, adds to the authenticity of your writing, helping readers to engage with the tale on a deeper level. You explore the currents of reality, guided by the stream, picking and combining the pieces that will bring your imaginary universe to life.

You observe the transformational force of the current of combining real-world components by surrendering to it. It becomes the anchor that anchors your tale, instilling it with credibility and resonance. Your attention to detail, like the river, carves a route through your tale, perfectly merging real-world aspects with the imaginary tapestry you've constructed.

The continual, flowing rhythm of introducing real-world components guarantees that authenticity is seamlessly integrated into your work. The river transforms into your muse, shaping the ups and downs of your creative process. Its current acts as a bridge, allowing you to easily traverse between the worlds of fiction and reality, resulting in a story that seems authentic and relevant.

As you go down the river of adding real-world components, you will see how each bit of realism, each injection of authenticity, improves your tale. Real-world components give your characters, situations, and events a firm basis, helping readers to connect with them on a personal level. They give your story depth, complexity, and relatability, helping it resonate with readers' personal experiences. Readers get completely involved in the flow of the narrative, their emotions moved by the realism of the world you've built, reflecting the rhythm you've painstakingly crafted.

Incorporating real-world components into the flowing river alters the entire geography of your literary universe, creating a lens through which your tale smoothly unfolds. Reality's current becomes the driving force, altering readers' involvement and enhancing their connection to your fictional world.

Incorporating real-life aspects and authenticity into your work is akin to blending a continuous, flowing river of reality with the colourful landscape of your fictitious realm. Imagine submitting to this river's soothing current as it leads you through the rich tapestry of the actual world, infusing your work with a sense of reality and resonance.

Immerse yourself in the river, and you'll learn the art of combining real-world elements and authenticity—a talent that allows you to draw on the depth and complexity of reality to improve your narrative. The river transforms into a conduit, connecting you to a huge array of human experiences, civilizations, and surroundings. You become the explorer, expertly navigating these currents to capture the essence of authenticity and effortlessly weave it into your story.

You go on a mission to find the right balance between fantasy and reality by combining real-world components. The river becomes your source of inspiration, providing a plethora of unique events, places, and people. Each real-world aspect, like tributaries merging into the main channel, adds to the authenticity of your writing, helping readers to engage with the tale on a deeper level. You explore the currents of reality, guided by the stream, picking and combining the pieces that will bring your imaginary universe to life.

You observe the transformational force of the current of combining real-world components by surrendering to it. It becomes the anchor that anchors your tale, instilling it with credibility and resonance. Your attention to detail, like the river, carves a route through your tale, perfectly merging real-world aspects with the imaginary tapestry you've constructed.

The continual, flowing rhythm of introducing real-world components guarantees that authenticity is seamlessly integrated into your work. The river transforms into your muse, shaping the ups and downs of your creative process. Its current acts as a bridge, allowing you to easily traverse between the worlds of fiction and reality, resulting in a story that seems authentic and relevant.

As you go down the river of adding real-world components, you will see how each bit of realism, each injection of authenticity, improves your tale. Real-world components give your characters, situations, and events a firm basis, helping readers to connect with them on a personal level. They give your story depth, complexity, and relatability, helping it resonate with readers' personal experiences. Readers get completely involved in the flow of the narrative, their emotions moved by the realism of the world you've built, reflecting the rhythm you've painstakingly crafted.

Incorporating real-world components into the flowing river alters the entire geography of your literary universe, creating a lens through which your tale smoothly unfolds. Reality's current becomes the driving force, altering readers' involvement and enhancing their connection to your fictional world.

Integrating real-world aspects and authenticity into your writing is akin to smoothly navigating a continuous, flowing river of information, where the currents of reality mix with the creative currents of your tale. Consider submitting to the smooth stream of this river as it leads you through the vivid tapestry of the actual world, filling your work with truth and resonance.

Immerse yourself in the flowing river, and you'll learn the art of combining real-world components and authenticity—a talent that will allow you to draw on the depth and complexity of reality to enrich your narrative. The river acts as a conduit, transporting you to a wide range of human experiences, civilizations, and environments. You take on the role of explorer, expertly navigating these currents in order to capture the spirit of authenticity and effortlessly weave it into your story.

You go on a mission to find the right balance between fantasy and reality by combining real-world components. The river becomes a source of inspiration for you, providing a wide range of real and relevant components. Each real-world aspect, like tributaries merging into the main channel, adds to the authenticity of your work, immersing readers in a universe that seems genuine and true. You explore the currents of reality, guided by the stream, carefully picking and integrating the components that will enhance your imaginary universe.

You observe the transformational force of the current of combining real-world components by surrendering to it. It serves as the basis for your tale, infusing it with a feeling of believability and resonance. Your attention to detail carves a path through your tale, effortlessly merging real-world things with the tapestry of your imagination, just as the river carves a path through the environment.

The continual, flowing rhythm of introducing real-world components guarantees that authenticity is seamlessly integrated into your work. The river transforms into your muse, shaping the ups and downs of your creative process. Its current functions as a bridge, allowing you to easily move between the realms of reality and fantasy, resulting in a story that has a tremendous impact on readers.

You see how each bit of fact, each injection of authenticity, strengthens your tale as you navigate the river of combining real-world material. Real-world components serve as a touchstone for readers, encouraging them to connect meaningfully with the characters, places, and events. They give your story depth, substance, and relatability, making it feel grounded and alive. Readers are completely involved in the flow of the tale, their emotional engagement heightened by the realism of the universe you've built, echoing the rhythm you've painstakingly established.

Incorporating real-world components into the flowing river alters the entire geography of your literary universe, providing readers with a lens through which to experience the tale. Reality's current becomes the driving force, molding readers' involvement and building a stronger connection to your fictional world.

Accept the art of combining real-world elements and authenticity, and allow the river to lead you on a profound creative trip. Allow the mobility of reality to influence and develop the authenticity of your tale. Allow your readers to be captivated by the river of real-world components, encouraging them to immerse themselves in a continuous, flowing torrent of words that resonates with the strength, authenticity, and immersive aspects of a brilliant tale.

Avoiding Common Pitfalls and Errors

Avoiding frequent traps and blunders is like to navigating a continuous, flowing river of writing wisdom, where the currents of knowledge direct you away from perilous rocks and hidden obstructions, allowing your words to flow freely and naturally. Consider submitting to the soothing stream of this river as it transports you on a voyage of writing greatness, guiding you away from frequent pitfalls and traps that might stymie your art.

Immerse yourself in the flowing river, and you'll learn the art of avoiding frequent traps and errors—a talent that will help you to gracefully traverse the twists and turns of the writing process. The river serves as your guide, providing you with a plethora of ideas and skills learnt by seasoned authors who have traveled this journey before you. You take on the role of explorer, expertly navigating the currents to protect the integrity and quality of your work.

You go on a mission to lift your writing to new heights while avoiding typical mistakes and faults. The river becomes a source of knowledge, revealing potential problems and flaws in your job. These teachings, like flags along the riverbed, serve as warning signals, pushing you to make wise decisions and avoid mistakes that might diminish the impact of your work. You sail the currents of wisdom, guided by the stream, learning from the experiences of others and applying those lessons to your own work.

You observe its transformational force when you surrender to the current of avoiding typical traps and blunders. It serves as a compass for your writing, steering you away from clichés, poor characterisation, uneven pacing, and other typical pitfalls. Your attention to detail, like the river, carves a course through your narrative, ensuring that it avoids the traps that might diminish its promise.

The continual, flowing rhythm of avoiding typical mistakes and faults guarantees that your work progresses smoothly. The river transforms into your instructor, molding the ups and downs of your creative process. Its present status serves as a protection, assisting you in identifying and correcting faults before they become obvious errors. The river becomes a valued companion, assisting your writing development and allowing your words to flow freely.

You can see how each lesson learnt, each avoided mistake, increases your writing as you cross the river of avoiding frequent pitfalls and blunders. Your writing improves, your characters become more interesting, and your storyline becomes more engaging. By eliminating frequent faults, you may create a more enjoyable reading experience for your readers, allowing them to become fully involved in the narrative's flow. Readers, too, are guided by the stream of the river, and their interest is enhanced by the absence of distractions and blunders.

Avoiding frequent hazards and blunders within the flowing river alters the whole landscape of your writing journey, ensuring that your words traverse a clean and unobstructed way to your readers' hearts and minds. The flow of insight becomes the driving force, moulding readers' attachment to your work and helping them to fully appreciate the creativity and talent you bring to your writing.

Avoiding frequent mistakes and blunders is akin to expertly navigating a continuous, flowing river of writing expertise, where the currents of knowledge gently guide you away from potential stumbling blocks and mishaps, allowing your words to glide easily towards perfection. Consider succumbing to the calm stream of this river as it guides you down a smooth path toward a polished and refined writing style.

Immerse yourself in the current, and you'll learn the art of avoiding frequent mistakes and errors—a talent that will allow you to sail through the writing process with confidence and grace. The river becomes your constant companion, providing a continual flow of thoughts and lessons gained from seasoned authors who have faced and conquered similar obstacles. You take on the role of the explorer, expertly navigating the currents to avoid the traps that might stymie your progress.

You go on a mission to lift your writing to new heights while avoiding typical mistakes and faults. The river becomes a source of wisdom, pointing out the pebbles and dangers that might undermine the effect of your work. These teachings, like subtle reminders along the riverbanks, act as guideposts, encouraging you to make mindful decisions and avoid the pitfalls that might weaken the quality of your work. You traverse the currents of wisdom, guided by the stream, absorbing the teachings of seasoned authors and applying them to your own work.

You observe its transformational force when you surrender to the current of avoiding typical traps and blunders. It becomes your compass, guiding you and ensuring the integrity of your writing. Your attention to detail, like the river, carves a path through your tale, ensuring that it is clear of the traps that might distract from its impact and cohesion.

The continual, flowing rhythm of avoiding typical mistakes and faults guarantees that your work progresses smoothly. The river becomes your guide, directing the ups and downs of your creative process. Its current serves as a safety net, letting you to notice and correct problems before they become major roadblocks. The river becomes a valued ally, assisting your writing development and allowing your words to flow freely.

You can see how each lesson learnt, each hurdle avoided, refines your writing as you navigate the river of avoiding frequent traps and blunders. Your language becomes more incisive, your storyline more fascinating, and your characters more believable. By eliminating typical mistakes, you produce a more fluid reading experience that allows readers to become fully absorbed in the narrative's flow. Readers, too, are guided by the stream of the river, and their interest is enhanced by the absence of distractions and blunders.

Avoiding frequent hazards and blunders within the flowing river alters the entire landscape of your writing trip, ensuring that your words transit a clean and unobstructed course to resonate with readers. The current of wisdom becomes the driving force, forming readers' connections to your work and helping them to recognize your skill and workmanship in writing.

Avoiding frequent traps and blunders is like deftly navigating a continuous, flowing river of writing wisdom, where knowing currents gently direct you away from perilous rocks and hidden obstructions, allowing your words to flow freely and naturally. Consider submitting to the soothing stream of this river as it transports you on a voyage of writing greatness, guiding you away from frequent pitfalls and traps that might stymie your art.

Immerse yourself in the flowing river, and you'll learn the art of avoiding frequent traps and errors—a talent that will help you to gracefully traverse the twists and turns of the writing process. The river becomes your trusty companion, providing a continual flow of thoughts and lessons gained from seasoned authors who have walked this route before you. You take on the role of the daring explorer, expertly navigating the currents to protect the integrity and quality of your work.

You go on a mission to lift your writing to new heights while avoiding typical mistakes and faults. The river becomes a source of wisdom, revealing the perils and mistakes that might jeopardize your effort. These teachings, like signposts along the riverbed, serve as beacons, reminding you to tread carefully and avoid mistakes that might distract from the brilliance of your writing. You sail the currents of wisdom, guided by the stream, learning from the experiences of others and applying those lessons to your own work.

You observe its transformational force when you surrender to the current of avoiding typical traps and blunders. It serves as a compass for your writing, steering you away from clichés, poor character development, uneven pacing, and other typical problems. Your attention to detail, like the river, carves a course through your narrative, ensuring that it avoids the traps that might diminish its promise.

The continual, flowing rhythm of avoiding typical mistakes and faults guarantees that your work progresses smoothly. The river becomes an ally, influencing the ups and downs of your creative process. Its present status serves as a protection, assisting you in identifying and correcting faults before they become obvious errors. The river becomes a constant friend, assisting your writing development and allowing your words to flow freely.

As you navigate the river of avoiding frequent pitfalls and blunders, you will see how each lesson learned and trap avoided enriches your writing. Your writing improves, your characters grow more developed, and your storyline becomes more interesting. By eliminating frequent faults, you may create a more enjoyable reading experience for your readers, allowing them to become fully involved in the narrative's flow. Readers, too, are guided by the stream of the river, and their interest is enhanced by the absence of distractions and blunders.

Avoiding typical traps and faults within the flowing river alters the entire landscape of your writing journey, ensuring that your words follow a clean and unobstructed course to capture readers. The tide of wisdom acts as a driving force, moulding readers' attachment to your work and helping them to appreciate the elegance and craftsmanship you bring to your writing.

Accept the art of avoiding typical mistakes and blunders, and let the flowing river to transport you on a transforming writing journey. Allow knowledge to mold and polish your writing by surrendering to its flexibility. Allow the river of knowledge to lead you, avoiding frequent traps that might stymie your art and allowing your words to flow freely, attracting readers with their clarity, depth, and impact.

Chapter 11: Editing and Revising Your Work

The Importance of Self-Editing

The value of self-editing is analogous to a gentle stream carrying your writing along a continuous, flowing river of refinement, where currents of examination and revision mould your words into a polished and compelling form. Consider submitting to the river's rhythmic flow as it takes you through the process of self-evaluation and progress, allowing your work to achieve its full potential.

Immerse yourself in the flowing river, and you'll discover the art of self-editing—the ability to critically examine your own work and make required changes. The river becomes your instructor, delivering a constant flow of opportunity to develop your thoughts, hone your language, and improve your narrative. You become the astute editor, expertly managing the currents to turn your rough work into a masterpiece.

You go on a path of self-discovery and refinement inside the fluidity of self-editing. The river becomes your mirror, reflecting back to you your writing with clarity and honesty. It allows you to take a step back from your job and look at it from a different angle. You traverse the currents of self-criticism, guided by the stream, recognizing places for development and making intentional decisions to better your work.

Surrendering to the current of self-editing allows you to experience its transformational force. It becomes the shaper of your writing, ensuring that every word, sentence, and paragraph is deliberate and effective. Your attention to detail, like the river, carves a route through your story, eradicating inconsistencies, clarifying concepts, and raising the overall quality of your work.

The continual, fluid rhythm of self-editing guarantees that your work progresses smoothly. The river becomes an ally, assisting your development as a writer. Its existing state serves as a guide, assisting you in identifying areas that need improvement, such as narrative gaps, weak characterizations, or repetitive language. The river becomes a source of inspiration for you, fuelling your desire to improve and perfect your work.

You can see how each rewrite, each moment of self-reflection enriches your work as you traverse the river of self-editing. Your language gets more exact, your thoughts become more cohesive, and your storytelling becomes more powerful. By embracing self-editing, you release the potential contained inside your first draft, allowing your work to shine with polished brilliance that captivates readers.

The necessity of self-editing creates the landscape of your writing trip inside the flowing river, ensuring that your words traverse a clear and captivating course. The current of self-examination becomes a driving force, pushing you to improve your writing talents and produce your finest work. It instills a feeling of discipline and craftsmanship in your writing, propelling it to new heights.

The value of self-editing might be compared to a steady, continual flow of refining that passes through your work, smoothing rough edges and improving overall quality. Consider submitting to the flow's rhythmic momentum, where every word and syllable becomes a chance for refinement and clarity.

Immerse yourself in the flowing river, and you'll acquire the art of self-editing—a necessary ability that will allow you to be your own critic and champion for your work. The river becomes your guide through the process of self-reflection and refining. You become the astute observer, expertly managing the currents to guarantee your work is flawless.

You go on a path of self-improvement and progress within the fluidity of self-editing. The river becomes like a mirror, reflecting your words back to you objectively and honestly. It provides a new viewpoint, allowing you to take a step back and evaluate your work from the standpoint of the reader. You traverse the currents of self-assessment, discovering areas of weakness and executing adjustments to improve your work, guided by the stream.

Surrendering to the current of self-editing allows you to experience its transformational force. It transforms into the purifying force that enhances your work, ensuring that each word has weight and each phrase flows smoothly. Your attention to detail, like the river, carves a route through your narrative, removing inconsistencies, tightening sentences, and increasing the power of your message.

The continual, fluid rhythm of self-editing guarantees that your work progresses smoothly. The river becomes an ally, assisting your development as a writer. Its current state serves as a guide, assisting you in identifying areas that require more care, such as grammar and punctuation, sentence structure, or concept clarity. The river becomes a source of inspiration, boosting your desire to improve and perfect your work.

You can see how each rewrite, each moment of inspection, enriches your work as you traverse the river of self-editing. Your writing sharpens, your storytelling becomes more interesting, and your thoughts become more cohesive. By embracing self-editing, you liberate the power of your words, allowing your work to shine with brilliance that captivates readers.

The necessity of self-editing creates the landscape of your writing trip inside the flowing river, ensuring that your words traverse a clear and captivating course. The stream of self-improvement becomes a driving force, pushing you to sharpen your talents and produce your finest work. It promotes discipline and skill, allowing you to take your writing to new heights.

The value of self-editing is like a river that passes through your work, slowly refining and sharpening it to perfection. Consider submitting to the river's calm, flowing stream, where every word, phrase, and paragraph becomes a chance for progress and refinement.

Immerse yourself in the flowing river, and you'll acquire the art of self-editing—a crucial ability that allows you to critically examine and improve your own work. The river becomes your guide, gently urging you towards a better understanding of the strengths and limitations of your work. You take on the role of the discriminating editor, expertly navigating the currents to unearth hidden treasures and smooth rough edges.

You go on a transforming path of self-improvement as a writer inside the fluidity of self-editing. The river reflects your creative voice, providing insights and revelations that help you to fine-tune your ideas and art. You traverse the currents of self-analysis, guided by the stream, assessing your work with a critical eye and making intentional decisions to increase its effect.

When you succumb to the stream of self-editing, you notice its deep impact on your work. It becomes the guiding force that develops and sharpens your work, ensuring that every word is meaningful and every phrase rings true. Your attention to detail, like the river, carves a route through your narrative, smoothing transitions, removing repetitions, and enhancing the overall structure of your writing.

Self-editing's constant, flowing rhythm assures a smooth evolution of your thoughts and message. The river becomes your colleague, assisting you in your writing development. Its current version serves as a mentor, assisting you in identifying areas that need improvement, such as character consistency, story coherence, or narrative pace. The river becomes a source of inspiration, fuelling your devotion to your trade and motivating a never-ending quest of greatness.

You can see how each correction, each moment of introspection, improves your work as you traverse the river of self-editing. Your language improves, your storytelling improves, and your voice becomes more unique. By accepting self-editing, you liberate the power of your words, letting them to flow naturally and attract readers with their beauty and impact.

The necessity of self-editing alters the entire landscape of your writing trip, ensuring that your words travel a clear and purposeful course within the flowing river. Self-improvement becomes the driving force, moving you to mastery and allowing your writing to shine clearly. It fosters a feeling of discipline and workmanship in your work, elevating it to new heights.

Accept the skill of self-editing and allow the river to transport you on a transforming writing trip. Allow improvement to mold and enhance your writing by surrendering to its flexibility. Allow the river of self-reflection to guide you through the currents of editing and refining, allowing your words to flow freely, attracting readers with their clarity, depth, and resonance.

Techniques for Strengthening Plot, Characters, and Language

Techniques for improving plot, characters, and language flow together like linked streams into a continuous, flowing river of narrative greatness. Consider submitting to the soothing stream of this river as it takes you on a voyage of creative mastery, helping you to polish and improve the key aspects of narrative.

Immerse yourself in the flowing river, and you'll discover a plethora of approaches that can help you take your writing to the next level. Each stream symbolizes a different part of storytelling, smoothly blending to make a unified story. The storyline flow is full of twists and turns that move your story ahead with suspense and excitement. The character stream is rich in depth and realism, bringing your heroes and supporting characters to life. The language stream sparkles with literary techniques, adding vivid imagery and lyrical beauty to your text.

You go on a voyage of creative empowerment inside the flexibility of these approaches. The river serves as your guide, providing a continual flow of thoughts and methods to help you improve your story, characters, and language. You become the expert navigator, expertly navigating the currents to strengthen the fundamental roots of your tale.

The plot stream encourages you to experiment with tactics such as creating a captivating story arc, creating fascinating conflicts, and effectively timing your narrative. It inspires you to write thrilling scenes, surprising twists, and gratifying endings. As the plot's momentum takes you, you construct a narrative environment that captivates readers and keeps them anxiously flipping pages.

The character stream encourages you to investigate strategies for bringing your characters to life. It supports the development of complex characters with strengths, faults, and intriguing motives. You learn how to write realistic conversation, foster character growth and change, and create emotional connections between your readers and the characters in your tale.

The language stream urges you to polish your prose, to use words that elicit emotions, paint vivid pictures, and arouse the senses. It exposes you to the power of figurative language, such as metaphors and similes, and walks you through the process of mastering descriptive storytelling. You learn how to modify sentence structure, generate rhythm and cadence, and infuse your work with a distinct voice that readers will recognize.

These interwoven streams mingle within the moving river, mingling and affecting one another. The plot stream drives the development of your narrative and the subtleties of your language, whereas the character stream influences the development of your plot and the nuances of your language. In response, the language stream heightens the impact of the story and enriches the characters.

Techniques for improving story, characters, and language flow together in a continuous, flowing river of narrative greatness. Imagine immersing yourself in this river of narrative mastery, where the currents of creative empowerment gently transport you on a voyage of creative empowerment, helping you to improve and strengthen the important parts of your writing.

As you succumb to the current, you'll uncover a plethora of tactics that will merge to take your narrative to new heights. Each approach symbolizes a stream that is intertwined with the others to generate a unified narrative flow. The narrative stream erupts with unexpected twists and turns, moving your story ahead with pace and interest. The character stream is rich, bringing depth, authenticity, and relatability into your heroes and supporting characters. The language stream glistens with literary techniques, dazzling with metaphors, vivid imagery, and poetic phrases, adding beauty and impact to your work.

You begin on a transforming journey driven by the currents of creative mastery inside the fluidity of these approaches. The river becomes your tutor, providing a steady stream of thoughts, methods, and tools to help you improve your story, characters, and language. You become the expert navigator, expertly navigating the currents while sharpening and refining the core of your tale.

The plot stream encourages you to experiment with skills like creating intriguing story arcs, weaving rich subplots, and expertly timing your narrative. It motivates you to write stories with building tension, dramatic climaxes, and rewarding conclusions. You construct a compelling environment that enthralls readers, keeping them actively engaged from beginning to end as you navigate the story stream.

The character stream encourages you to investigate strategies for bringing your characters to life. It encourages you to create fully developed persons with distinct personalities, desires, and conflicts. You investigate techniques for producing realistic dialogue, revealing inner thoughts and feelings, and constructing connections that are appealing to readers. The character stream adds dimension to your writing by allowing your readers to identify with the characters in your tale.

The language stream urges you to polish your prose, to choose words that elicit emotion, stimulate the senses, and leave an indelible imprint. It encourages you to experiment with metaphors, similes, and other literary elements that will enrich and texture your writing. The language stream invites you to experiment with sentence constructions, use vivid descriptions, and develop your own unique voice, infusing your words with strength and resonance.

These interwoven streams combine and intermingle inside the moving river, affecting and strengthening one another. The plot stream molds your characters' growth and conflicts, whereas the character stream accelerates the development of your narrative and determines your language choices. In turn, the language stream enhances the impact of your story and develops the characters.

Techniques for improving plot, characters, and language flow together like a river of narrative greatness, guiding your work to its maximum potential. Consider succumbing to the soft currents of this river, where the currents of storytelling craftsmanship combine perfectly, moving your story forward with precision and impact.

Immerse yourself in the flowing river, and you'll find a plethora of ways that can help you improve your writing. Each approach is a tributary that joins forces to generate a unified narrative flow. The narrative tributary swells with enthralling twists, turns, and climax moments, ensuring your story moves forward with exciting momentum. The character tributary runs deep, bringing your protagonists and supporting cast to life and allowing readers to relate deeply with their travels. Literary tropes, figurative language, and evocative descriptions abound in the linguistic tributary, immersing readers in a vibrant and intriguing universe.

You go on a revolutionary journey of creative mastery inside the fluidity of these approaches. The river becomes your guide, providing a steady flow of thoughts, methods, and tools to help you improve your story, characters, and language. You become the expert navigator, skillfully navigating the currents while polishing and perfecting your narrative talents.

The plot tributary encourages you to experiment with strategies like creating well-structured story arcs, creating interesting conflicts, and keeping a balance of suspense and rhythm. It motivates you to provide stakes, shocks, and resolves that will keep readers interested and wanting more. You construct a dynamic narrative environment that captivates and resonates as you navigate the story tributaries.

The character tributary encourages you to research strategies for bringing your characters to life. It encourages you to develop complicated personalities, motivations, and connections that play out naturally throughout the tale. You investigate techniques for creating character arcs, constructing interesting conversation, and eliciting genuine emotions in your readers. The character tributary adds depth to your writing by making your characters feel genuine and sympathetic.

The language tributary invites you to polish your work by choosing words that create imagery, engage the senses, and elicit emotional reactions. It encourages you to use literary elements like metaphors, similes, and symbols to create a complex and engrossing reading experience. The language tributary pushes you to employ rhythm in your sentences, precise and vivid descriptions, and to develop a distinct writing style that will create an impression on your readers.

These interwoven tributaries combine and harmonize inside the flowing river, each affecting and enriching the other. The plot tributary creates your characters' journey, whereas the character tributary drives the development of your narrative and affects your language choices. In turn, the linguistic tributary amplifies the effect of both storyline and character, engaging readers in a rich and captivating tale world.

Accept the approaches for enhancing story, characters, and language, and let the river to transport you on a transforming writing trip. Allow narrative greatness to mold and enhance your skill by surrendering to its flexibility. Allow the currents of story development, character depth, and linguistic skill to lead you as you navigate the river of creative mastery. And, as your words flow with ease, engage readers with a story that transports, enlightens, and stays in their hearts and minds, leaving an everlasting mark on their reading journey.

Seeking Feedback and Working with Editors

Seeking comments and working with editors is like starting a never-ending conversation that improves the depth and quality of your writing. Consider immersing yourself in this dialogue's dynamic stream, where the ebb and flow of cooperation and feedback propels your work to new heights.

Immerse yourself in the flowing river, and you'll realize how important criticism and cooperation are in your writing journey. Each contact is a moment of connection in which you share your work with others and ask their feedback. The river acts as a channel, allowing for a constant flow of ideas, insights, and constructive criticism that drives your progress as a writer.

You go on a journey of development and refinement inside the fluidity of this interaction. The river serves as a sounding board, offering a welcoming environment for you to share your work and receive crucial feedback. You transform into the inquisitive learner, open to taking comments and welcoming the possibility for progress.

The feedback stream encourages you to seek out different points of view, and it welcomes comments from trustworthy peers, writing groups, or industry pros. It encourages you to be open to constructive criticism, perceiving it as a chance to improve your work and increase its effect. You obtain insights into areas that need additional development as you navigate the feedback stream, whether it's story coherence, character consistency, pace, or thematic depth.

The collaboration stream encourages a collaboration between the writer and the editor, in which their experience and insights combine to form and develop your work. It entails a continual interchange of ideas, comments, and edits that contribute to your writing's overall power and clarity. The collaboration stream encourages you to put your faith in an editor's experience, respecting their advice as they guide you through the currents of revision and improvement.

You observe the transformational power of feedback and cooperation when you surrender to their current. They act as development accelerators, broadening your creative horizons and challenging you to stretch the boundaries of your work. Feedback and participation create your narrative in the same way as the river carves its route through the terrain, allowing your tale to expand and bloom.

The ongoing cycle of refinement and enhancement is ensured by the continuous, flowing rhythm of soliciting input and working with editors. The river becomes an ally, assisting you in your writing progress. Its latest version provides new viewpoints, assisting you in identifying blind spots, strengthening weak areas, and celebrating your abilities. The river becomes a source of inspiration for you, boosting your ambition to improve and perfect your work.

You see how each encounter, each moment of connection, improves your work as you navigate the river of criticism and cooperation. It turns into an iterative process of sharing, learning, and adopting improvements that improve your job. By accepting the thoughts and skills of others, you unlock your writing's full potential, infusing it with clarity, coherence, and resonance.

The notion of requesting input and working with editors affects the whole geography of your writing trip, ensuring that your words traverse a clear and engaging course within the flowing river. Collaboration becomes a driving force, forcing you toward constant growth and allowing your writing to shine brilliantly. It promotes openness, adaptability, and a dedication to excellence.

Seeking feedback and working with editors is like being immersed in a never-ending dialogue that improves the quality and impact of your writing. Consider entering a river of collaborative discussion, where currents of insight and knowledge mold and enhance your work, guiding you to brilliance.

You learn the incredible importance of criticism and participation in your writing journey as you immerse yourself in the flowing river. Each engagement serves as a link between you and others, allowing for the exchange of ideas, points of view, and constructive criticism. The river serves as a channel for this discussion, fostering ongoing development and progress.

You go on a revolutionary path of perfecting your craft inside the flexibility of this discourse. The river transforms into a welcoming area, enabling you to share your work and receive crucial feedback. You become the enthusiastic participant, ready to learn, adapt, and broaden your creative horizons.

The feedback current encourages you to seek out other points of view, and it welcomes input from reliable sources such as peers, writing groups, or specialists in the subject. It encourages you to be receptive to constructive criticism, acknowledging that it is a helpful tool for improving your work. As you navigate this current, you get insights into your writing's strengths and flaws, indicating areas that need to be improved, whether it's story coherence, character depth, or narrative rhythm.

The present cooperation encourages a partnership between the writer and the editor, a symbiotic interaction in which their experience and insights combine to improve the overall quality of your work. It entails a continuous interchange of ideas, comments, and changes, all of which contribute to the development and polishing of your work. The collaboration mode enables you to put your confidence in your editor's skills as they guide you through the seas of revision and improvement.

Surrendering to the flow of feedback and cooperation allows you to see their transformational potential. They act as growth accelerators, broadening your creative horizons and driving you to achieve new heights in your work. Feedback and cooperation build your narrative, shaping it into a captivating and profound work, much as the river carves its route across the terrain.

The constant, flowing rhythm of seeking input and collaborating with editors provides a never-ending cycle of refinement and advancement. The river becomes your ally, assisting you on your writing trip. Its present state offers new insights, shedding light on areas that require work, emphasizing your abilities, and encouraging you to strive for perfection. The river becomes a source of inspiration for you, boosting your dedication to your profession and encouraging you to polish and perfect your writing.

You observe the transforming impact of each encounter as you navigate the river of feedback and cooperation. It becomes an iterative process of sharing, learning, and applying adjustments that give your writing new life. You may unleash the full potential of your work by embracing the thoughts and skills of others.

The notion of seeking input and working with editors affects the whole geography of your writing journey within the flowing river. It guarantees that your words follow a clear and engaging course, capturing readers' attention with their depth and strength. The current of cooperation becomes the driving force, moving you forward and allowing your writing to shine brightly. It cultivates an open, adaptable, and steadfast dedication to excellence.

Seeking feedback and collaborating with editors is like immersing yourself in a river of never-ending discussion that develops and refines your writing. Consider immersing yourself in this dynamic river, where the currents of cooperation and feedback push you toward improving your skill.

You recognize the great worth of criticism and participation in your writing journey as you immerse yourself in the flowing river. Each contact becomes a fluid interchange of ideas, thoughts, and viewpoints, flowing in unison with the stream of the river. The river itself acts as a conduit, allowing for a steady flow of information and assistance to assist you in improving your work.

You go on a revolutionary path of development and progress within the fluidity of this discussion. The river becomes your collaborator, giving a welcoming environment in which to share your writing and receive crucial feedback. You become an active participant, relishing the chance to learn, adapt, and grow as a writer.

The feedback current motivates you to seek out different points of view, soliciting comments from fellow authors, beta readers, or writing clubs. It encourages you to welcome constructive criticism, knowing that it is a necessary component of progress. As you navigate this current, you get insights about your writing's strengths and shortcomings, allowing you to precisely tweak and polish your work.

The contemporary partnership develops a bond between writer and editor, resulting in a seamless combination of skill and vision. It entails a constant dialogue that shapes and enhances your writing. The present partnership encourages you to put your confidence in the editor's advice, enabling their expertise to lead your edits and changes. You see the transforming power of teamwork as you navigate this current, as the editor's skill improves the clarity, coherence, and impact of your work.

You observe the beauty they produce by surrendering to the flow of feedback and cooperation. They become improvement catalysts, driving you to explore new ideas and strive for greatness. Feedback and cooperation change your work, polishing it into a fascinating, polished piece of art, just as the river carves its route through the landscape.

The constant, flowing rhythm of seeking input and collaborating with editors provides a never-ending cycle of refinement and advancement. The river becomes a valued companion, accompanying you on your writing trip. Its current brings new ideas, moving you forward and encouraging you to push yourself. The river becomes a source of inspiration for you, fuelling your dedication to your profession and motivating you to always polish and perfect your work.

You experience the power of each encounter as you navigate the flow of feedback and cooperation. It becomes an iterative process of sharing, listening, and applying adjustments that give your writing new life. By accepting the thoughts and skills of others, you unlock the full potential of your work, producing a story that has a strong emotional resonance with readers.

The notion of requesting input and working with editors affects the landscape of your writing journey within the flowing river. It guarantees that your words flow easily and effectively, capturing readers' attention with their clarity and impact. Collaboration becomes the driving force, pulling you forward and allowing your writing to shine brightly. It promotes an open, adaptable, and unwavering pursuit of greatness.

Accept critiques and collaborate with editors, and let the flowing river transport you on a transforming writing trip. Accept the flow of the discourse and the great insights it provides. Allow the river of cooperation and feedback to lead you, allowing you to navigate the currents of revision and improvement. And, when your words flow with ease, capture readers with a story that displays your passion, progress, and unshakable commitment to the craft of writing.

Conclusion

Congratulations on finishing this incredible trip through the realm of creative writing! As you near the end of this book, pause to consider the richness of information and inspiration you've gained along the road. You've become a writer, armed with an arsenal of skills, insights, and a burning desire to tell stories that will leave an everlasting impact on your readers' hearts and minds.

Remember that writing is a lifetime discipline that requires constant development and refining. Accept the power of your imagination, which has no limitations. Allow your imagination to run wild on the page, bringing to life bright people, thrilling stories, and captivating settings. Allow your words to flow like a river, enthralling readers with your distinct voice and the depth of passion you inject into each line.

Develop the value of discipline and regularity as you begin your writing adventure. Make time in your day to develop your trade, since it is only through constant practice that the beauty of creation may bloom. Accept the ebb and flow of inspiration, relying on personal experiences, watching the environment around you, and using prompts to spark your creativity as necessary.

Make your characters with care, giving them life and a sense of purpose. Allow them to express themselves via meaningful discourse, their words resonating with sincerity and depth. Lead them via transforming character arcs and motives that will captivate readers.

Construct sophisticated storylines that keep readers on the edge of their seats by weaving conflict, tension, and plot devices into each page. Infuse sensory elements into your surroundings to take readers to the heart of your narrative, eliciting emotions and immersing them in a world of wonder.

Master the technique of employing point of view to captivate readers and enhance their relationship with your characters. Create a personal writing style that represents your particular voice, employing figurative language and literary methods that build vivid pictures in your readers' imaginations.

Edit and revise with zeal, refining your work until it gleams. Seek feedback from reliable sources, appreciating their views and implementing their suggestions to improve your narrative skills. Collaborate with editors, acknowledging their enormous worth in turning your work into a polished beauty.

Remember that your path is as unique as your voice as you traverse the huge ocean of creative writing. Accept the obstacles and rejoice in the victories since they are the stepping stones to your development as a writer. Exhibit the endurance, resilience, and unrelenting enthusiasm that distinguishes exceptional artists.

Now, equipped with this book's information, tactics, and inspiration, go forth and let your imagination fly. Paint worlds with your words, touch hearts with your stories, and leave an indelible mark on those who journey with you via your writing.

May your pen never dry up, and may your stories shine brightly in the broad realm of writing. Happy writing, and may your creative activities offer you contentment, joy, and the satisfaction of knowing that your words have the potential to inspire and alter people.